YOU DON'T NEED TO FIND G-O-D

God Explained in Plain Language

JAMES FINKE

You Don't Need a Ph.D. to Find G-O-D:
God Explained in Plain Language by James Finke.

© 2021 by James Finke

Published by Living Sacrifice Books, LLC

Cover design by Brooke Baker

Every effort has been made by the author and publisher to ensure that the information contained in this book was correct as of press time. The author and publisher hereby disclaim and do not assume liability for any injury, loss, damage or disruption caused by errors or omissions, regardless of whether any errors or omissions result from negligence, accident, or any other cause. Readers are encouraged to verify any information contained in this book prior to taking any action on the information.

For rights and permissions, contact:

Living Sacrifice Books, LLC.
authorjamesfinke@gmail.com

CONTENTS

PART 1: SCIENCE
CHAPTER 1: *Big Bang* 9
CHAPTER 2: *Goldilocks* 13
CHAPTER 3: *Play Ball* 19
CHAPTER 4: *Eighth Wonder* 25
CHAPTER 5: *"I Believe In Science"* 31

PART 2: PHILOSOPHY
CHAPTER 6: *Right And Wrong* 39
CHAPTER 7: *Human Rights* 47

PART 3: COMING INTO FOCUS
CHAPTER 8: *Who Is Jesus?* 59
CHAPTER 9: *Batting 1,000* 65

PART 4: GOD'S WORD
CHAPTER 10: *He's Been There All Along* 75

PART 5: THE GOOD NEWS
CHAPTER 11: *The Wedding Cake Worldview* 83

PART 6: I DON'T WANT IT TO SEEM LIKE I'M QUESTIONING, BUT
CHAPTER 12: *FAQ's* 93

PART 7: CONCLUSION
CHAPTER 13: *Course Correction* 119
CHAPTER 14: *The Place Of Victory* 123

CHAPTER 15: *Your Turn* *125*
Resources For A Deeper Dive *127*
About The Author *129*

NOTES

Looking for more biblically based encouragement? You can sign up for James' **free** *Good News Only Friday* newsletter here: Click Here to Subscribe.

Httpsː//www.authorjamesfinke.com
Httpsː//www.facebook.com/authorjamesfinke
Httpsː//www.instagram.com/authorjamesfinke

INTRODUCTION

You Don't Need a Ph.D. to Find G-O-D

God Explained in Plain Language

My wife is a social worker by trade. I'm in the insurance business, so when she and her social worker friends talk shop, it can actually sound like a foreign language to me. "*I checked on the QRC, but his DZM was ABC.*" You probably know the feeling. It could be mechanics talking cars, doctors discussing a procedure, whatever. If it's not your trade, they might as well be speaking Greek. You end up smiling and nodding, ready to move on to the next subject.

Does talking about God make you feel like an outsider listening to others "talk shop"? I'm convinced it is the case for many, whether or not they believe that God actually exists.

This is for you.

I'm not a pastor. I didn't go to seminary. Nor am I a professional scientist. Indeed, I've studied their work, but I couldn't write with their perspective even if I wanted to. It's kind of like, having a friend who's really into basketball. He may know his stuff, but he still isn't going to be slam-dunking if he's 5'2. I'm just a "regular guy" with the same fundamental question as you: **How do I find God?** The answer to that one question impacts and unlocks everything else in this life:

Is there a purpose for my life? Is there an afterlife? Will I someday see my friends and relatives again that have passed away? What religion is "right"? Is there a right and wrong way to live? Should I be going to church?

Now, most people accept that it takes faith to believe in God. But do you realize that it also requires faith to believe that there is no God? Faith is "the evidence of things we cannot see."[1] Right in the definition, we see that faith isn't meant to be blind. Just as our muscles can grow stronger through exercise, our faith to believe or not believe, can grow stronger through the study of the evidence.

This book is the result of my own study of the evidence. I've read, and I've listened to everything I could get my hands on from the top experts in the field. Experts in science, philosophy, history, religion, communication, and even crime investigation.

I've boiled it down and will share my takeaways as only a "regular guy" can. For example, I'll reference expert scientific research, but we won't get bogged down in hyper-technical scientific discussion. I'll also avoid using religious terms that would likely be foreign to those outside of the church.

I'm giving you the bottom line here and will share sources you can use to dive deeper into any of the topics we hit. If you want to know the intricacies of the second law of thermodynamics or to explore deep anagogical hermeneutics, there are plenty of places you can get that; it just won't be in this book.

Are you ready? Let's talk God.

---

[1] Hebrews 11:1 NKJV

PART 1
SCIENCE

CHAPTER 1

BIG BANG

> *The Big Bang Theory is how astronomers explain the way the universe began. It is the idea that the universe began as just a single point, then expanded and stretched to grow as large as it is right now (and it could still be stretching).*
> *-Spaceplace.nasa.gov*
>
> *"I believe in the Big Bang. I just know who banged it."*
> *-Dr. Frank Turek*

Have you ever wondered how our world started?

Science has proven that our universe exploded into being out of nothing. That means everything; including space, time, and matter didn't exist. There was absolutely nothing, and then; Bang! There was something.

But we didn't always know that. Even Albert Einstein originally believed that the universe itself was eternal. In other words, the universe was always "just there" with no beginning and no end. Think about what that would mean. If it were always "just there," then the universe wouldn't have needed something or someone to have created it. If it was always "just there," then perhaps somehow our world began by accident. You see, when we accept something as "just there," we don't really think about how it got to be that way.

Here's a thought experiment to show you what I mean. Something that we consider "just there" in our day to day lives is gravity. Now gravity does some pretty awful things. It causes planes to crash. It caused my son to knock out his front tooth before his first birthday while learning to walk. And yet, no one ever complains about gravity. Have you ever heard someone tell you that they were having a great day until gravity kicked in and ruined things? Of course not. Why? *It's just there.*

Thanks to modern science, we now know that our universe isn't actually eternal. It was *not* always "just there." There's a wide range of evidence that proves so; but let's focus on the discovery that changed Einstein's mind. In 1929 Edward Hubble discovered the expansion of the universe. Einstein initially rejected the theory that the universe was expanding. That was until Hubble invited Einstein out to look through his telescope in Mount Wilson, California. The rest is history. Einstein later went on to say that his greatest professional mistake was an effort to prove that the universe was "just there" and not expanding.

Okay. The universe is expanding from a central point. So what?

Takeaway #1 is that the universe had a cause. If the universe is expanding from a central point, it had a beginning, and if it had a beginning, it had a cause. Someone or something caused it! It wasn't always "just there."

So the options we are left with are as follows:

1. If there is a God: God caused the universe to explode into being, out of nothing.
2. If there is no God: Nothing caused the universe to explode into being, out of nothing. [2]

---

[2] I Don't Have Enough Faith to be an Atheist, Chapter 3, Frank Turek & Norm Geisler

I don't need to be Einstein to know that option two makes very little sense. But perhaps you're thinking; couldn't it have been something other than God? Here's the thing, there was nothing else. Science has proved that all space, time and material exploded into being, out of nothing. Therefore, the cause of the universe has to be something **outside** of time, space and material. What could exist outside of time, space, and material? An eternal God.

Fellow spreadsheet nerds rejoice! As we walk through this evidence, we'll organize our takeaways by building a simple comparison spreadsheet.

God	No God
God caused the universe to explode into being, out of nothing.	Nothing, caused the universe to explode into being, out of nothing.

CHAPTER 2

GOLDILOCKS

> *First, she tasted the porridge of the Great Big Bear, and that was too hot for her. Next, she tasted the porridge of the Middle-sized Bear, but that was too cold for her. And then she went to the porridge of the Little Wee Bear and tasted it, and that was neither too hot nor too cold, but just right, and she liked it so well that she ate it all up, every bit!*   -Goldilocks and the Three Bears

One morning recently, rather than being at work as I normally would be, I found myself at a walk-in medical clinic waiting to be tested for Covid-19 (coronavirus). Eight months ago, that sentence wouldn't have made sense to many people, but I trust you know what I'm talking about as our country approaches 140 million Covid tests administered since then.

After registering inside, I was instructed to wait outside of the building until I received a text message. That would be my notice to come back inside and be tested. I checked the list and had about 50 people ahead of me. Yes, there was a high demand for the privilege of having a large q-tip jammed up both nostrils on a Monday morning. I was going to be there a while.

With time to kill on a beautiful day, I decided to go for a walk. A mid-day walk on a Monday? That's a rare pleasure for someone who spends much of their day during the week indoors working, on a computer.

The weather was flawless. Sunny, with a slight cool breeze. Totally comfortable to walk around in with a t-shirt and jeans. It was perfect. So perfect, in fact, that I went out of my way to check the temperature.

For the record: seventy-two degrees. Seventy-two and sunny with a slight breeze is my "Goldilocks" weather. Not too hot, not too cool, but *just* right. Like it was made especially for me.

Do you realize that we're living in a "Goldilocks" universe, too? Not too hot, not too cool, but *just* right. Like it was made especially for us. This leads us to our next takeaway.

Takeaway #2 is that the universe is "tuned up" to allow life.

When I tune-up my guitar and play a chord, it rings out beautifully, just as I intend it to. I turn the knobs at the top of the guitar until all six strings are set to the sound they're designed to be. This is not a "horseshoes and hand grenades" situation where the goal is to be "close enough." No, I use an app on my smartphone to make sure the strings are *precisely* tuned to the levels they should be. Any guitarist will tell you that if any one of those six strings is out of whack in either direction, it can ruin the entire sound. So I adjust the knobs until each string is not too tight, not too loose, but *just* right.

If I don't tune up the guitar, it sounds awful. Immediately, I know something is out of whack. But do you know what would give me an even more clear warning than a poor sounding chord? What if the guitar instantly burst into flames or went into a tailspin and exploded if it wasn't tuned up? Or if even one string was ever so slightly out of tune, whether it was too tight or too loose, the guitar froze over and disintegrated.

Sound dramatic right? Maybe so, but that's nothing compared to the fine-tuning of our universe!

There are dozens of constants, like gravity, oxygen levels, and nuclear force; these things had to be set to extremely precise parameters for Earth to be habitable. Forget about tuning just six strings, if any of these dozens of constants were even **slightly** different, our world could not exist. Life could not exist. What does "slightly different" look like? Consider this example:

If you stretched a tape measure across the entire known universe, mark it on one spot. That would be the correct calculation for gravity. If this mark were moved more than an inch from its location (on a tape measure stretched across the entire universe!), our world could not exist. [3]

Am I to believe that precise specification happened by accident? And that's just one of the dozens of factors that had to be tuned precisely to the right level to allow life. If the Earth were closer to or further from the sun, we wouldn't be here. If oxygen made up more or less than 21% of the atmosphere, we wouldn't be here.[4] If the Earth's rotation took more or less than 24 hours, we wouldn't be here. If the Earth were tilted more or less than at a 23-degree angle, we wouldn't be here. Finally, it should be noted that these factors are interdependent. If I break one string on my guitar, it also throws off the other five strings' settings.

It's truly difficult to comprehend just how miraculously "tuned up" our universe is. And yet, we know it to be so. It's this type of information that led Francis Collins, the Yale-educated scientist and Director of the National Institutes of Health, to famously say that *"The more I examine the universe and the details*

---

[3] Stealing from God, Chapter 1, Frank Turek

[4] I Don't Have Enough Faith to Be an Atheist, Chapter 4, Frank Turek and Norm Geisler. Paraphrased.

of its architecture, the more evidence I find that the universe in some sense must have known we were coming.[5]"

Chapter 1 confirmed that our universe exploded into being, out of nothing. Through that explosion, a universe formed that is tuned up to ultra-precise levels needed to allow life. How do we explain this without God?

Some have tried to explain it away with a theory that there is an unlimited number of universes and that we happened to be on the one that happened to have the exact interdependent constants needed to allow life. With that in mind, I'd like to devote the next page of this book to lay out the evidence for this theory.

---

[5] The Language of God: A Scientist Presents Evidence for Belief; Francis S. Collins

This page intentionally left blank.

I don't need to be a molecular geneticist to tell you that my guitar strings don't accidentally get tuned up. Given any number of chances, if we put the raw materials into a box and dropped them out a window, we'd never believe the result of that explosion to be a perfectly tuned guitar.

So, we're again left to consider our options:

3. If there is a God, our universe is tuned up for life because God tuned it.
4. If there is no God, our universe is tuned up for life because nothing caused a lucky accident.

God	No God
God caused the universe to explode into being, out of nothing.	Nothing, caused the universe to explode into being, out of nothing.
God tuned up the universe to allow life.	Nothing, caused a lucky accident that tuned up the universe to allow life.

CHAPTER 3

PLAY BALL

Baseball has a language of its own, featuring at-bats, bloopers, chin music, dingers, errors, force outs, going yard, homers, infield flies, jacks, K's, lineups, middle relievers, no-hitters, outfielders, pop flies, quick pitches, RBI's, southpaws, triples, upper decks, visiting teams, windups, yips, XBH's and zones.

It's no surprise that the sport known as "America's Pastime" since the late 1800s has become a part of the lexicon across virtually every aspect of our culture. Even those with little to no interest in baseball would understand whether an event was a "home run" or if someone "struck out." You may not need the exact price upfront but would be willing to settle for a "ballpark figure." Or if a close friend needed your help, you'd probably be willing to "go to bat" for them. Finally, you might be expecting one thing only to have someone "throw you a curveball" and surprise you.

The spoken language of baseball permeates our culture. And yet, what is fascinating is that every baseball game also features an *unspoken* language used to deliver messages throughout the game from the first pitch until the final out. This language may be much less obvious to the casual observer, yet it is critical to every baseball game. We're talking about **signs**.

At any one time, there are upwards of nineteen people in motion on the baseball field during a game. There are nine fielders on defense, one batter and up to three runners on offense, two base coaches, and four umpires. Keep in mind, that only includes those *on the field.* Each team also has a dugout housing a manager, assistant coaches, and a total of 25 players on the active roster. I wasn't a math major, but I can tell you that all of these numbers add up to one thing; *communication.*

Like anything else in life, the ability to communicate during a baseball game often distinguishes those who are successful from those who suffer defeat. A strategy is required to choreograph the action on the field, and therefore instructions must be delivered throughout the game.

So why is much of this instruction delivered via "unspoken" messages? Consider this:

A batter steps up to home plate and awaits the first pitch. The catcher hollers out to the pitcher, "Our scouting report says that this guy has trouble hitting a curveball. Let's throw him a curveball outside and see if we can get him to swing and miss". Meanwhile, the base coach for the offense is hollering to the batter, "Swing away at the first pitch!" Finally, the pitch is thrown. Since the batter knows which pitch is coming, he waits on the curveball and hits it hard. The fielders must try to throw the ball to first base before the batter gets there. It's a very close call, but the umpire is yelling that the batter is "safe." Unfortunately, the crowd is roaring because it was a close play. Neither the fielders nor the crowd knows what the ruling is.

As you can see, some verbal communication during the game just won't cut it. Leonard Schechter of the New York Post compared a batter that knew what pitch was coming to "the driver who knocks down an 89-year old pedestrian. It's easy but unsporting."

Teams can gain a strategic advantage if they can silently deliver instructions without the opposing team intercepting those messages. Let's revisit our example and replace verbal communication with the silent language of baseball.

A catcher choreographs the defense on a baseball field much like a conductor choreographs an orchestra. His position involves squatting down behind the batter and shielding his hand, so the opponent can't see it. He and the pitcher have a prearranged code system. One finger signals a fastball, two fingers signal a curveball, and three fingers signal a changeup. He shows two fingers, signaling for the curve. The pitcher nods in agreement. With the pitch set, the catcher slides over toward the outside of the strike zone to signal where he wants the pitch thrown.

The infielders also know this code system. They see that the pitch is a curveball and that the catcher is setting up toward the outside of the strike zone. Accordingly, they shift their positions in the direction that the batter is most likely to hit the ball. The infielders also flash a hand signal to pass the message along to the outfielders, who are too far away from the catcher to see the original sign.

With no words spoken, the entire field of nine defensive players know what pitch is coming next and where the ball is most likely to be hit. They shift their positions to put themselves in the best spot to get the batter out.

While all of this is happening, the offensive team has its own stream of communication. The manager in the dugout is communicating with the coach that is out on the field. That coach is then delivering signs to the batter and any runners who are on base.

Finally, after the ball is hit and the play is made, it's up to the umpire to rule whether the batter is safe or out. Rather than relying on voice alone, the umpire signals "safe!" stretching out both arms horizontally with hands open. Both teams, the other umpires, and the entire crowd instantly know the call.

Deciphering codes in the name of gaining a strategic advantage is a critical part of the game. Consider how much information, how many instructions are delivered silently within this play, and keep in mind that this all occurs during **one pitch** of the game. An average Major League baseball game has approximately 294 pitches thrown and runs over 3 hours long.

During the course of an average baseball game, there are upwards of **1,000** silent instructions given and received.[6] These signs vary from team to team and even from player to player. These codes can be changed regularly, whether it be to different signals or different meanings. The gestures can vary in every conceivable way, and yet, there is one common thread that ties *all* of these signs together.

> *The element common to 100% of the signs given during a baseball game is that they all come from minds.*

I am yet to hear a baseball player report that they were told to swing at a pitch by their baseball bat. I am yet to hear of a baseball glove that instructed a fielder what their assignment was on a given play. Mindless matter has never been observed to create messages, even simple messages.

Takeaway #3 is that instructions require intelligence.

Scientists call DNA the **instruction** book of life. The chemicals in DNA literally make up a genetic alphabet, which encodes instructions for building and replicating all living things. In other words, DNA is not just chemicals. It's a language and it is unimaginably complex. For example, the instructions written in this genetic alphabet for a "simple" single-celled amoeba are the equivalent to the amount of information in 1,000 encyclopedias[7]. And this isn't random information. It's in a

---

[6] The Hidden Language of Baseball, Introduction, Paul Dickson
[7] I Don't Have Enough Faith to Be an Atheist, Introduction, Frank Turek and Norm Geisler

specific order that makes up the unique genetic makeup of that living thing.

If we know inherently, that a simple code like two pointed fingers which signifies a curveball requires a mind to design it, how much more so would that apply to a complex code? The DNA code within every person, if laid out end to end, would go to the sun and back numerous times. Matter is unable to create a code system.

If we know inherently that even simple instructions require a mind to design them, how much more so would that apply to complex instructions? There are 10 BILLION miles of DNA instruction in all the cells of your body.

Am I to believe that mindless chemicals somehow produced the instructions? In other words, the book for life wrote itself. I'm yet to hear of a bag of sunflower seeds that sent a strategic message to a baseball coach.

Again we are left to consider our options:

1. If there is a God, the instruction book for life (DNA) was designed by God.
2. If there is no God, the instruction book for life made itself and is written by mindless chemicals.

God	No God
God caused the universe to explode into being, out of nothing.	Nothing, caused the universe to explode into being, out of nothing.
God tuned up the universe to allow life.	Nothing, caused a lucky accident that tuned up the universe to allow life.
God designed D.N.A., the unimaginably complex instruction book for life.	Mindless chemicals blindly produced D.N.A., the unimaginably complex instruction book for life.

CHAPTER 4

EIGHTH WONDER

> *"Compound Interest is the eighth wonder of the world. He who understands it earns it. He who doesn't pays it. Compound interest is the most powerful force in the universe." -Albert Einstein*

"If you understand this one concept by the time you leave this class tonight, you can retire as a millionaire."

I still remember the looks on their faces. It was a mix of goofy grins, and some healthy "are they for real?" skepticism. My wife and I were teaching a personal finance class to a group of High Schoolers. Our lessons were based on principles from books like Chris Hogan's "Everyday Millionaires" and Thomas J. Stanley's "Millionaire Next Door." We'd been through foundational teachings about discipline and how having nice stuff does not automatically mean that someone is wealthy. That outward appearance of nice stuff is often a mask, hiding a mountain of credit card debt, leased cars, and student loans. Debt will take away your freedom.

Things are not always as they seem. In fact, most millionaires are not at all what you may picture. Most High Schoolers picture professional athletes and movie stars flying around on private jets when they think "millionaire." Or trust fund kids who inherited their wealth. The truth is that they probably know a typical "Millionaire Next Door" and have no idea they're wealthy. They are teachers, engineers, business owners, accountants, and the likes. Most did not inherit their money. Rather they've avoided debt, paid off their homes, and invested in their 401k/retirement accounts. Instead of trying to impress others, they've simply lived on less than they've earned for a long period of time. That's how they got to be millionaires! And most of them are able to do this, on a modest income. You don't need to make a million dollars a year to become a millionaire. Most never even earn $100,000 in a year[8].

So with this foundation laid and the kids' interest piqued, we turned our attention to the concept that leads to a millionaire retirement. It's what Einstein called the "eighth wonder of the world": **compound interest.** We showed them that if a teenager will be disciplined and start investing at a young age, even if it's not a lot of money, they can harness the power of compound interest. Time is on your side. This is the antithesis of a "get-rich-quick" scheme. So how exactly does it work?

As Benjamin Franklin put it, "Money makes money. And the money that money makes, makes money."[9] In other words, we are talking about **small incremental change over a long period of time.** Each year the amount snowballs, so if you start investing early, your 401k retirement account can look much different at age 65 than it does at age 25. It can grow exponentially, and surely some of the parts that make up the account would change over time. But do you know what *doesn't change*, whether it's a $2,000 account or a $2.2M account?

It's still a 401k retirement account. There is a difference between changes *within a type* and changing from one type to another. In other words, compound interest can grow a 401k dramatically, but it doesn't turn it into a block of gold, or a

---

[8] Everyday Millionaires, Chris Hogan

[9] Benjamin Franklin and Compound Interest: "Money makes money. And the money that money makes, makes money" — My Money Blog

rental property, or a piece of art. This leads us to our next takeaway:

Takeaway #4: there is a difference between microevolution (changes within a type) and macroevolution (changing from one type into another).

Charles Darwin's Theory of Evolution essentially says this: there is no God. The world and all living things appear to be designed, but there is no designer. Rather, there is one "common ancestor," probably a one-celled creature, that has evolved into the millions of different species of living things on Earth over time. This is often depicted as a tree, with the trunk's bottom being the simplest creatures who evolved into more complex creatures and branched out into new species over millions of years. Variations in traits arise *randomly*, and by the survival of the fittest, those traits are passed down to future generations. The changes must be made slowly through small incremental change because any large or rapid changes would be mutations and would ultimately lead to death. By this natural selection process, one single-celled creature has "evolved" into all other living beings on the planet.

Here's the thing: **this type of evolution has NEVER been observed. Survival of the fittest has never been observed to create** *new types.*[10]

What has been observed is called Microevolution. Microevolution refers to adaptations that occur *within* a species. In contrast, Macroevolution is the unproven assumption that one species can evolve into another by natural processes alone. There is no reason to believe that, if given

---

[10] I Don't Have Enough Faith to be an Atheist, Chapter 6, Frank Turek and Norm Geisler

enough time, the observed adaptations within a species would cause them to change into a new species.

That's not all; because Darwin's theory assumed one simple creature evolved over millions of years by tiny changes, there would have to be "transitional creatures" as one species evolved into another. So if Darwinism were true, we would have found, (1) the earliest creatures to have been very simple and (2) transitional creatures that gradually appear over millions of years.

The actual fossil record tells a very different story. Darwin sent a copy of his book to Louis Agassiz, a Harvard-trained scientist and the top authority on the fossil record at the time. Agassiz rejected the theory based on the fossil record. Now fast-forward to today[11]. If Darwinism were true, we would have found thousands, if not millions, of transitional fossils by now. That hasn't happened[12]. The fossils that have been found cause yet another problem for Darwinism; they indicate that a huge variety of sophisticated creatures appeared suddenly. Fossil discoveries such as the "Cambrian Explosion" troubled Darwin because they show complex creatures appeared suddenly at the dawn of life, with no evidence of simpler ancestral forms of these creatures. The variety of these complex creatures were so extreme that it took decades for paleontologists to grasp it fully[13]. Stephen Meyer details this challenge to Darwin Macroevolution in his book "Darwin's Doubt."

Darwin's response in the late 1800s was essentially that we needed more time to discover more fossils. As science has become more sophisticated and discoveries have been made,

---

[11] Darwin's Doubt, Chapter 1, Stephen Meyer

[12] I Don't Have Enough Faith to be an Atheist, Chapter 6, Frank Turek and Norm Geisler

[13] Darwin's Doubt, Chapter 2, Stephen Meyer

macroevolution looks less likely than ever. Also, if blind evolution were true, how did it know to stop with humans? Wouldn't humans continue evolving into new species?

Generally, scientists that seek to support the unproven assumption of macroevolution point to a common genetic code as the best evidence for macroevolution. However, as discussed in chapter 3, information requires intelligence. Thus it is much more probable that rather than one common ancestor, DNA points to one common C*reator.*

I'm yet to hear of a 401k account that changed type into a block of gold by "natural processes," let alone a species that changed type by "natural processes" alone.

Finally, let's put aside for a moment all of the evidence against it and assume that macroevolution was actually true. That still doesn't explain what caused the universe to explode into being out of nothing, how our world is miraculously tuned up to allow life, or how mindless chemicals wrote the instruction book for life, D.N.A. Whether or not evolution occurred, it doesn't explain how the first life came to be. The first dollar for that 401k account still has to come from somewhere before it can grow and change over the years. In other words, if macroevolution were somehow true: so what? That still would not disprove God.

As always, we're left to consider our options,

1. If there is a God, macroevolution appears false but doesn't disprove God even if it were true.
2. If there is no God, macroevolution appears false but must be true and must also disprove God.

God	No God

God caused the universe to explode into being, out of nothing.	Nothing, caused the universe to explode into being, out of nothing.
God tuned up the universe to allow life.	Nothing, caused a lucky accident that tuned up the universe to allow life.
God designed D.N.A., the unimaginably complex instruction book for life.	Mindless chemicals blindly produced D.N.A., the unimaginably complex instruction book for life.
Microevolution exists. Macroevolution appears false because it is.	Macroevolution appears false but must be true and must somehow account for the first life.

CHAPTER 5

"I BELIEVE IN SCIENCE"

It's happened to just about everyone. You're stuck in traffic on the highway, inching your way along due to a car accident. But by the time you get to the scene of the accident, you realize it didn't even happen on the side of the highway you're traveling on. The lanes you're traveling on aren't blocked at all. Rather, the traffic is caused by drivers in your lane "rubbernecking" to get a better view of the wreck that occurred across the median on the other side of the highway and as annoyed as we might be, we can't help but glance over and examine by ourselves, what happened. Why do we do this?

When we witness a car accident or hear an awful story on the news, our "fight or flight" response kicks in. We know we aren't imminently in danger, but just seeing danger can cause us to confront the fears we hold. Hence the phrase "It was like a car accident. I couldn't look away."

Recently I was playing tennis and overheard a conversation happening amongst players on an adjacent court. In short, one of the players was mocking her friends for a belief in God. I didn't want to be distracted from an intense match with my Dad and brothers, but the conversation was like a car accident. I couldn't stop listening.

> *"You really think there's some God out there just creating a universe? You really think there's a heaven? I don't believe in God. I believe in science and stuff."*

Yes, it was a pretty deep conversation to be having in between games and I was taken aback. I knew the so-called "war between science and religion" existed amongst keyboard warriors on social media, but I was startled to hear it play out in person. It was particularly disturbing because the players, by my best guess, had to have been high school age.

It's an odd thing to hear someone cite a "belief in science" as evidence against a belief in God. Indeed, the takeaways we've established thus far are largely drawn from things we've learned about the universe using the scientific method. In other words, saying science somehow disproves God is like saying that there can't be an author to the book because you learn by reading. The idea that one would need to choose between science and God doesn't hold water.

Science is often portrayed as a completely unbiased process of simply observing facts. But it's important to remember something I first heard from Dr. Frank Turek: "Science says absolutely nothing. Scientists say something". In other words, every scientist is a human, and so, therefore, they have a worldview and pre-conceptions[14].

Takeaway #5 is that science says nothing. Scientists say something.

Dr. Turek explains that the debate between science and God really isn't a debate over evidence at all. In most cases, we're all dealing with the same evidence. It is really, a debate over philosophy. For example, many scientists who do not believe in God rule out supernatural causes ahead of time. So even if

---

[14] Science Doesn't Say Anything-- Scientists Do (crossexamined.org)

scientific evidence points to a cause outside of time, space and matter, a scientist who does not believe in God must not follow the evidence there. They must continue searching for a "natural" cause. The irony is that this "belief in science" requires blind faith; the precise accusation often leveled at people for believing in God. Rather, belief in God allows a scientist to follow the evidence wherever it leads them[15].

A further irony is that modern science was largely developed by people who were motivated to study nature *because* they believed in God. For instance, Isaac Newton, the scientist who discovered gravity when an apple fell and hit him on the head, viewed God as a great engineer. Galileo, considered the father of modern science, said, "We cannot presume to know how God thinks; we must go out and look at the world He created." He viewed God as a divine craftsman[16].

Think about it. If you believed there was no God, why would you expect there to be coherent laws across the entire universe you could study? Copernicus, who discovered that the sun was the center of the universe rather than Earth, wasn't dealing with new evidence or new ways to observe the stars. Rather, he was driven to this discovery by believing that the universe is mathematical and orderly because a rational God created it[17].

A belief in science with no God has massive philosophical implications, similar to those that would apply to a belief that humans are essentially blindly evolved apes. We'll review this further in the next section, but as always, I leave you to consider our options:

---

[15] I Don't Have Enough Faith to be an Atheist, Chapter 12, Frank Turek and Norm Geisler

[16] The Soul of Science: Christian Faith and Natural Philosophy, Nancy R. Pearcey and Charles B. Thaxton

[17] The Soul of Science: Christian Faith and Natural Philosophy, Nancy R. Pearcey and Charles B. Thaxton

1. If there is a God, science is a process we use to learn about the universe God created.
2. If there is no God, science is a religion unto itself. The possibility of a miracle must be ruled out ahead of time.

PART 1 REVIEW

Let's review what we know.

1. The universe had a cause.
2. The universe is tuned up to support life.
3. Instructions require intelligence.
4. There is a difference between microevolution and macroevolution.
5. Science says nothing. Scientists say something.

These takeaways must be explained, so we compare worldviews:

God	No God
God caused the universe to explode into being, out of nothing.	Nothing, caused the universe to explode into being, out of nothing.
God tuned up the universe to allow life.	Nothing, caused a lucky accident that tuned up the universe to allow life.
God designed D.N.A., the unimaginably complex instruction book for life.	Mindless chemicals blindly produced D.N.A., the unimaginably complex instruction book for life.
Microevolution exists. Macroevolution appears false because it is.	Macroevolution appears false but must be true and must somehow account for the first life.
Science is a process we use to learn about the universe God created.	Science is a religion unto itself.

PART 2
PHILOSOPHY

CHAPTER 6

RIGHT AND WRONG

> *"The only way you know that a line is crooked is because you have a concept of what straight is." -CS Lewis.*[18]

A filibuster is a political procedure where one or more members of congress debate over a proposed piece of legislation to delay or entirely prevent a decision being made on the proposal. Explained another way, a filibuster is what happens every night at my house when it's bedtime for the kids. One night recently, part of my daughter's strategy was to tell me about what she'd learned in school that day. Sure, she'd been home for about six hours and waited until it was bedtime to share this vital information, but it ended up being a fascinating conversation. She proudly explained:

> *"Daddy, if I say purple is the best color, that's called my opinion. Because my friends could say that blue is the best color. But if I say 2 + 2 = 4, that's a fact, because it's true for everybody."*

---

[18] Mere Christianity, CS Lewis

Even in first grade, we recognize that opinions come from people. An opinion can only exist if a person thinks it. However, some universal truths do not come from people. These universal truths are valid and binding for everyone, whether or not the individual agrees with them. They would even be true if there were no one on the planet.

Whether or not an individual or group accepts it, two plus two equals four for everyone at all times. Even if the planet were uninhabited, would two apple trees plus two pear trees still not equal four trees? That's why we say that math is discovered, not invented. **The laws of mathematics aren't created by people.** They're real and exist on their own.

Conversely, would "I think purple is the best color" still be true if no one is on the planet? Of course not. That requires you, a person, to be there to think it.

So to summarize:

Opinion	I think purple is the best color.	True for me only, not binding for anyone else.	Requires a person to think it to exist.	Created by humans.
Universal Truth	2 + 2 = 4	True for everyone, even if an individual doesn't accept it.	Still true if no one were on the planet.	Discovered by humans.

Now consider these statements:
1. Torturing babies for fun is morally wrong.
2. Molesting children is morally wrong.
3. Racial discrimination is morally wrong.
4. Terrorism is morally wrong.

Are these "I think purple is the best color" opinion statements? Or are these "2 + 2 = 4" universal truths?

Let's test them. First, are they true for everyone, whether or not an individual accepts them? Absolutely. Think about a psychopath who actually does think torturing babies, molesting children, discriminating based on race, or committing terrorism is fun. Maybe their upbringing or culture gave them the idea that these things were okay. Perhaps even their government promoted these things (think Nazi Germany). Do we give them a pass because their personal opinion is that it's acceptable? Or are there universal moral truths that say these things are wrong, whether or not an individual accepts it?

Secondly, would the statements still be true even if no one were on the planet? They certainly would because they are universal truths. Therefore, just as math is real and exists on its own, universal moral truths are also real and exist on their own. Just as mathematics laws are discovered, not invented by people, moral laws are not invented by people too.

Takeaway #1 is that moral laws are like the laws of mathematics. People do not invent them, yet they apply to everyone. They would be true even if there were no one on the planet.

Consider what this means. Moral laws essentially describe a code of conduct for people: what is right and what is wrong. This analysis tells us that we have a code of conduct that is not invented by people but is valid and binding for all people. This moral code of conduct requires a moral code giver. We must decide which worldview makes more sense of this reality:

God	No God
God is the moral code giver.	What is right and wrong is just a matter of personal opinion.

While this concept may sound new to you, it's not. You inherently know that God's moral code of conduct exists and applies to everyone. In fact, you use this code of conduct anytime you disagree with someone else on a moral value. God's moral code of conduct serves as an **unchanging standard** that all actions can be measured against. Think of it like this:

If your watch says it's 1:30 PM and my watch says it's 1:35 PM, who's watch is correct? Both could be wrong, but we know both cannot be right at the same time. Your opinion is that your watch is accurate. My opinion is that my watch is accurate. So, how do we settle this?

We need to refer to a standard that transcends both watches. In other words, a standard **outside** of both watches. So we would compare our watches with the UTC (Coordinated Universal Time), which is the official basis for civil time today. If we left it up to the individual watches, it would ultimately come down to your opinion against mine. We know that both watches can't be right at the same time, but what makes your opinion any more valid than my opinion of the time?

The way to solve this is that we need a universal standard outside of the individual watches to compare it to. We check the external standard and whoever's time is synced up with the standard is correct.

Now instead of the time, let's insert a moral issue. Person A believes that abortion is acceptable, while Person B believes that abortion is murder. Both cannot be right simultaneously, and neither of us believes it's just a matter of your opinion against mine. If it were, what would make one opinion any more valid than anyone else's? No, the way to solve this is to refer to a universal standard outside of humanity. Whether or not we even realize it, we both inherently seek to measure our actions against God's universal standard that applies to everyone.

Takeaway #2 is that anytime you disagree with someone else's moral values, you're acknowledging that there is an unchanging standard outside of humanity that applies to everyone.

God	No God
God is the moral code giver.	What is right and wrong is just a matter of personal opinion.
God's moral code of conduct is the unchanging standard that all actions can be measured against.	You've never disagreed with anyone else's moral position on anything because it's just their personal opinion.

One way that people who don't believe in God try to explain God's moral code of conduct is to say that what is right and wrong is actually determined by what society deems acceptable. Sounds reasonable; but begs all sorts of questions like, which society? What if society has it wrong? What if the members of a society have radically different viewpoints on whether something is right or wrong?

Leon Trotsky was a Russian Revolutionary and a leader of the Bolshevik Party. He helped incite Russia's 1917 revolution with Vladimir Lenin and subsequently led the Soviet Union's Red Army. After Lenin died in 1924, Trotsky engaged in power struggle against Joseph Stalin and lost. He was pushed out of his roles and was ultimately expelled from the country in 1929. He lived the rest of his life in exile in various locations, including

Turkey, France, Norway and Mexico. While in exile, Trotsky continued to write and criticize Stalin.

On August 20th, 1940, Trotsky was attacked in his Mexico City home by Ramon Mercador, an undercover agent for the Soviet Union's secret police. Mercador got alone with Trotsky in his study and struck him from behind in the head with an ice axe, puncturing his skull. Mercador testified at his trial, "I laid my raincoat on the table in such a way as to be able to remove the ice axe which was in the pocket. I decided not to miss the wonderful opportunity that presented itself. The moment Trotsky began reading the article, he gave me my chance; I took out the ice axe from the raincoat, gripped it in my hand, and with my eyes closed, dealt him a terrible blow on the head." Trotsky died the next day[19].

The ramifications of Trotsky's assassination are fascinating. The murder was committed in Mexico. Therefore, Mercador was turned over to Mexican authorities and ultimately convicted for murder. He was sentenced and served twenty years in prison. He was released in 1960 and moved back to the Soviet Union in 1961. Upon his return, the head of the KBG presented Mercador with the country's highest civilian award, the Order of Lenin. This award was given for outstanding service to the State[20].

So which is it? In Mexico, the assassination was considered morally wrong and caused Mercador to become a convicted cold-blooded killer, while in Russia, that same act was considered morally right and earned him the title "Hero of the Soviet Union." Was the assassination moral or immoral?

---

[19] Leon Trotsky - Wikipedia
[20] Leon Trotsky - Wikipedia

Takeaway #3 is: Morality requires a standard outside of human opinion. That measuring stick is called God. Society is not outside of human opinion.

God	No God
God is the moral code giver.	What is right and wrong is just a matter of personal opinion.
God's moral code of conduct is the unchanging standard that all actions can be measured against.	You've never disagreed with anyone else's moral position on anything because it's just their personal opinion.
God is the measuring stick outside of human opinion.	"Society" is the measuring stick for what is right and wrong.

If good and evil are just human-made, then there is nothing truly good or truly evil. It's just a matter of opinion. Your opinion may be that smashing an old man in the head with an ice axe for political gain is wrong, but Joseph Stalin's opinion was that it was wonderful. Mexican society may say it's wrong, but Soviet society applauded it. Inherently we know there is a universal moral code that applies to all people beyond "you say tomato, I say tomahto."

If there is no God, then it's just your opinion against 7 BILLION other human opinions. And if it's just opinion, then you have no right to say your moral ideas are superior to anyone else's. Some people think that tragedies like the Holocaust, 9/11, and Sandy Hook were justified, understandable, or even heroic. If even one of those things is objectively wrong, God exists. If *anything* is objectively wrong, God exists.

CHAPTER 7

HUMAN RIGHTS

If you watch television shows on National Geographic, you're bound to see heinous crimes committed in broad daylight. On the plains of sub-Saharan Africa, a pack of cackling hyenas gang up on a wildebeest and brutally murder it. No sooner than these gang members murder the wildebeest that a large lion appears. The lion intimidates the hyenas and steals the carcass of the wildebeest. It's unconscionable. We're talking pre-meditated murder, assault, and larceny at a minimum.

And yet, the narrator calmly describes the action matter-of-factly. There is no outrage in his voice and no rush to bring the perpetrators to justice. How can that be? Simply put, because the participants haven't done anything wrong. Can you picture the lion lying on a psychologist's couch, hashing out the guilt he feels for stealing from the hyenas? Of course not. Chris Rock famously captured this sentiment in 2004 during a comedy show when he declared, "that tiger didn't go crazy, that tiger went tiger!"[21]

---

[21] HBO Special "Never Scared", Chris Rock

Takeaway #4 is that animals have no moral obligation to one another.

Indeed, there is nothing evil about what the lion did because animals owe no moral obligation to one another. We understand that. But if there were no God and humans were actually just animals that blindly and randomly evolved from a common ancestor, logic would tell us that we also have zero moral obligation to one another. And yet, we know that isn't the case. That's not consistent with reality. Of course, we have a duty to treat one another well.

This issue is often misunderstood to mean that if you don't believe in God, you're immoral. That's not the case, and it's not what I'm saying here. There are people of all different worldviews who live morally upright lives. The point is that the moral code we live by is evidence that a God exists, whether or not an individual *believes* in a God.

As we discussed in Part 1, the so-called "war between science and religion" continues to dissolve as science progresses. Science continues to point to a Creator, and this issue is no different. Whereas one-time, conventional wisdom indicated that babies were born as a "blank slate" and were taught right from wrong, researchers at Yale University's Infant Cognition Center now believe otherwise. Their decades of experience in studying babies' minds indicate that while our circumstances and experiences can shape our moral beliefs, we appear to be **born with a simple understanding of right and wrong.** In other words, we appear to be created with a moral code of conduct "hardwired" into our being[22].

1. If there is a God, we have moral obligations to one another because we were created to live under God's moral code of conduct.

---

[22] Are we born with a moral core? The Baby Lab says 'yes' (cnn.com)

2. If there is no God, we are "evolved" animals and therefore have no more moral obligation to one another than the hyenas do for the wildebeest.

Any parent can tell you that our children have an inherent sense of justice. For verification, simply give one child a full candy bar and their sibling half of a candy bar. They don't need to be taught that it's "not fair." They will protest the injustice virtually as soon as they're old enough to communicate.

God	No God
God is the moral code giver.	What is right and wrong is just a matter of personal opinion.
God's moral code of conduct is the unchanging standard that all actions can be measured against.	You've never disagreed with anyone else's moral position on anything because it's just their personal opinion.
God is the measuring stick outside of human opinion.	"Society" is the measuring stick for what is right and wrong.
We have moral obligations to one another because we were created to live under God's moral code of conduct.	We are "evolved" animals and therefore have no more moral obligation to one another than the hyenas do for the wildebeest.

This morning I was reading a newsletter that reports on issues relevant to the insurance industry. One of the leading stories of the day was "World's Strongest Storm in 2020 Kills at Least 16 in Philippines". The cover photo of the story showed people being evacuated before a typhoon hit. A soaked-to-the-bone worker in a hardhat holds a tarp above the head of a young girl to shield her from the pouring rain. The girl can't be more than 5 or 6 years old, and they are walking through what looks like a dilapidated slum. The girl's lips are pursed, and her eyes cut right through me as I view the photo.[23]

It hurt. It just didn't seem fair that she was going through such an awful situation. Something inside of me kept telling me that this is wrong even though:

- I know almost nothing about this young girl.
- She lives halfway across the globe, and I will almost certainly never meet her.
- I have no idea what type of life she's lived, what good or bad deeds she's done, etc.

I know almost nothing about this young girl, yet I inherently know that her life is precious. We don't need to be taught that all human life is precious. It's something we know naturally. **This little girl's life is precious, and it's not because she is a random accident of nature.** She is special simply because she is a person, and people are created by God. Inherently we know that value in a creation is derived based on its creator, like a painting from the brush of Pablo Picasso.

Takeaway #5 is: the existence of basic human rights assumes the existence of a Creator, God.

A belief in God is the foundation upon which basic human rights are built. The preamble to the UN Universal Declaration of Human Rights says as much:

---

[23] https://www.insurancejournal.com/news/international/2020/11/02/589132.htm

"Whereas recognition of the inherent dignity and of the equal and inalienable rights of all members of the human family is the foundation of freedom, justice and peace in the world,[24]"

Human rights exist based on the knowledge that there are inherent dignity and worth in all human life. The inherent dignity and worth come from a Creator, not from non-living chemicals that somehow randomly "evolved."

1. If there is a God, all human life is precious because God creates us.
2. If there is no God, humans are random accidents of nature.

But what about people whose actions seem to fly in the face of the inherent dignity of personhood? What about atrocities committed by groups like the Nazis? Throughout the course of history, groups have dehumanized their enemies to get past what they know to be wrong. The Nazis referred to Jews as rats during the holocaust, the Hutu's referred to the Tutsis as cockroaches during the Rwandan Genocide, and slaves have been considered sub-human throughout history[25]. We see this today as many supporters of abortion seek to dehumanize unborn babies.

---

[24] https://www.un.org/en/universal-declaration-human-rights/

[25] 'Less Than Human': The Psychology Of Cruelty : NPR

PART 2 REVIEW

Let's review what we know:

1. Moral laws are like the laws of mathematics. People do not invent them, yet they apply to everyone. They would be true even if there were no one on the planet.
2. Anytime you disagree with someone else's moral values, you're acknowledging that there is an unchanging standard outside of humanity that applies to everyone.
3. Just like the disagreement on time required a standard outside of the watches, morality requires a standard outside of human opinion. That measuring stick is called God. Society is not outside of human opinion.
4. Animals have no moral obligation to one another.
5. The existence of basic human rights assumes the existence of a Creator, God.

PART 3
COMING INTO FOCUS

What makes more sense to you?

God	No God
God caused the universe to explode into being, out of nothing.	Nothing, caused the universe to explode into being, out of nothing.
God tuned up the universe to allow life.	Nothing, caused a lucky accident that tuned up the universe to allow life.
God designed D.N.A., the unimaginably complex instruction book for life.	Mindless chemicals blindly produced D.N.A., the unimaginably complex instruction book for life.
Microevolution exists. Macroevolution appears false because it is.	Macroevolution appears false but must be true, and must somehow account for the first life.
Science is a process we use to learn about the universe God created.	Science is a religion unto itself.
God is the moral code giver.	What is right and wrong is just a matter of personal opinion.
God's moral code of conduct is the unchanging standard that all actions can be measured against.	You've never disagreed with anyone else's moral position on anything because it's just their personal opinion.
God is the measuring stick outside of human opinion.	"Society" is the measuring stick for what is right and wrong.
We have moral obligations to one another because we were created to live under God's moral code of conduct.	We are "evolved" animals and therefore have no more moral obligation to one another than the hyenas do for the wildebeest.
Human rights exist because all human life is precious. All human life is precious simply because it's Creator (God!) is special.	Humans are not specially created; they are accidents of nature.

Bottom line #1 is that the evidence proves that God exists. But who's God? Modern culture often treats religion as a spiritual "make your own Sundae" (pun intended), encouraging individuals to mix and match aspects of various faiths so God(s) can be whoever you want them to be. And don't all religions basically say the same thing anyway? A high-level review of the major world religions indicates that there are truth and goodness in virtually all of them. For example, the "golden rule" of treating others as you would want to be treated is expressed in Christianity, Confucianism, Buddhism, Hinduism, Islam, Judaism, and Taoism, among others[26]. Most world religions value ethical behavior, serving others, being a part of a community, taking responsibility for your actions, etc. There is a lot of common ground between them. **But there is also a lot of common ground between a bottle of wine and a bottle of grape juice, and no one would consider drinking them to be the same thing.**

Beyond just telling us that a God exists, the evidence we have, helps bring into focus a picture of who God is. For example, we know He isn't an impersonal force because He *chose* to create the universe and tuned it up for a purpose. Impersonal forces don't make choices. Gravity doesn't decide if it's in the mood to work that day. We also know that there aren't multiple gods out there. If there were a god of sun, a god of moon, a god of water, and so forth, would that make for an orderly place? Of course not. And yet, our entire understanding of the universe is built upon the fact that the universe *is* subject to orderly natural laws. **There is no scientific method without these laws.**

So we know that there is one true God who created the universe without even making reference to the Torah, the Bible, The Quran, or any other holy book. To sharpen our focus even more, we have to examine the fundamental difference

---

[26] teachingvalues.com

between Judaism, Christianity, and Islam. That fundamental difference can be summed up in one word: **Jesus.**

CHAPTER 8

WHO IS JESUS?

Who is Jesus? The Bible contains the story of Jesus' life and teachings. Multiple eyewitness accounts (known as the "gospels") tell of Jesus teaching the highest level of ethics known to humanity. He took moral virtues like "don't cheat on your spouse[27]" and elevated them to "if you even look at a woman lustfully, you've already committed adultery with her in your heart"[28]. And he himself never sinned. He performed miracles like healing a paralyzed man and giving sight to the blind. He forgave the sins of others. Even the waves and wind obeyed him as he calmed storms with his command. He claimed to have been in existence before the world began.

There have been many moral teachers and prophets throughout history, such as Moses, Buddha, Muhammad, and Confucius. These leaders claimed to hear from God, but that wasn't his case. Jesus didn't just claim to hear from God; he claimed to **BE** God in the flesh.[29] The religious and political leaders of the time considered his claim to be blasphemy. Jesus predicted his own death and claimed that after three days, He

---

[27] Exodus 20:14 NKJV paraphrased

[28] Matthew 5:28 NIV

[29] More than a Carpenter, Chapter 2, Josh McDowell and Sean McDowell

would rise again. Indeed, he was executed in the most shameful way possible because of who He said He was. They hung Him on a cross in between two criminals and even upon His death, He prayed, "Father, forgive them. They don't know what they're doing[30]". He died on that cross so that our sins could be forgiven and was taken off the cross and laid in a tomb.

His followers were heartbroken, scared, and scattered. They thought he was God in the flesh, but now their leader was dead, and they too, by association, were in danger. They stayed in hiding and eventually moved on with their lives, right?

Wrong!

Something changed. Within days of His execution, Jesus' followers were boldly proclaiming that Jesus was alive. They claimed that His tomb was found empty and that an angel in the tomb delivered the good news: "He is not here. He is risen!"[31]. They claimed that Jesus had appeared to them, that they'd eaten with him, that they'd touched him. They did this even though it caused them to be criticized, persecuted, tortured, and even killed. Eleven of Jesus' twelve closest followers (called apostles) were killed for preaching the good news of Jesus Christ after his death. Yet, no one ever recanted their testimony.

So we have to ask ourselves: who would die for something they knew to be a lie?[32] This wasn't hearsay; these were followers claiming they personally had spent time with Jesus after his death. These were men who lived the most ethical lives known. There was no financial gain to be had. Rather, the followers had every reason to deny that Jesus was alive. It makes no sense

---

[30] Luke 23:34 NIV

[31] Matthew 28:6 NKJV

[32] More than a Carpenter, Chapter 7, Josh McDowell and Sean McDowell

that someone would suffer persecution and death if they hadn't actually experienced the risen Jesus.

As explained by former cold-case homicide detective, J. Warner Wallace, it's important to understand that martyrdom unto itself doesn't prove something is true. For instance, the Islamic terrorists who hijacked the planes on 9/11 believed they were dying a martyr's death. But they died because they believed something from thousands of years earlier. In other words, they could have mistakenly believed something that wasn't true. **Jesus' followers who died were eyewitnesses.** They would know firsthand whether or not what they were dying for was true. Completely different situation[33].

Somehow there was a movement based on a man that had just been executed in the most shameful way possible. Over 10,000 people were converted in five weeks in a very hostile environment[34]. All the while, the enemies of Christianity could have stopped the movement in its tracks very simply. Jesus didn't predict that He would only spiritually rise again. He said He would **bodily** rise again. All they would have to have done was to produce the dead body of Jesus, and they couldn't do it. They never even disputed that the tomb was empty. That was common knowledge. They instead tried to claim His body was stolen.

There's a lot here, so let's review the facts:

1. **Fact**: Jesus was killed in the most shameful way possible because He claimed to be God in the flesh.
2. **Fact**: After seeing their leader killed, Jesus' followers were in hiding, scared for their lives.

---

[33] Cold-Case Christianity, Chapter 7, J. Warner Wallace

[34] Case for Christ, Chapter 14, Lee Strobel

3. **Fact**: Jesus' body was laid in a tomb. He had predicted he would rise again in three days, so guards were assigned to prevent disturbance of the tomb.
4. **Fact**: On the third day after he was killed, Jesus' tomb was found empty. The guards were terrified.
5. **Fact**: Jesus' followers came out of hiding, boldly proclaiming that the risen Jesus had appeared to them. That they'd eaten with him and touched him.
6. **Fact**: Jesus' followers had every reason to deny Jesus was alive. Claiming he was alive caused them to be persecuted and killed.
7. **Fact**: No one ever recanted their testimony despite interrogation and torture.
8. **Fact**: In the five weeks following Jesus' death, 10,000 were converted to Christianity in the midst of a very hostile environment.
9. **Fact**: The enemies of Christianity could have squashed the entire movement if they had produced the body of Jesus to prove he had not been bodily resurrected.
10. **Fact**: Today, over 2,000 years later, there are approximately 2.5 BILLION Christians alive who worship Jesus[35].

Takeaway #1 is that this fact pattern only makes sense if it's true! And if it's true, Jesus is God in the flesh. He willingly died for us and was risen on the third day. His followers suffered persecution, torture, and death for their faith in Jesus. But they never recanted their testimony because He appeared to them after His death. They ate with him and touched him. **Jesus is Lord.**

Some have tried to explain away the facts by claiming that the resurrection of Jesus is either an elaborate conspiracy theory or a myth. To this, we again reference J. Warner Wallace, a

---

[35] Christianity by country - Wikipedia

former cold-case homicide detective. He is an expert in conspiracy theories and explains that a successful conspiracy requires a small number of co-conspirators and a short conspiracy timespan. This makes sense. Three people are less likely to blow it, than 30 people. And there's a better chance of keeping a secret for 5 minutes than for 5 years. Taken to an extreme, the ideal conspiracy would be that two people commit a crime together, and one kills the other after it's over. Small group, short time period[36].

By this measure, the idea that Jesus' followers were lying about his resurrection from the dead is a horrible conspiracy theory. First off, the group is way too large-- the Bible details how Jesus appeared to over 500 followers. Am I to believe that over 500 followers were in on a lie and kept it a secret for over 60 years? That they somehow lined up their stories and no one recanted despite being scatted around the Roman Empire, interrogated and tortured? It makes no sense.

The idea that the resurrection of Jesus is a myth similarly wilts when we hold it up to inspection. Here's the main problem: myths don't develop while thousands of eyewitnesses are alive. You can't make up a lie when there are eyewitnesses there to refute it. That's why anytime you look through history; it takes centuries for myths to develop.

Takeaway #2 is that the reports of Jesus rising from the dead were written during eyewitnesses' lifetimes. These reports make up the New Testament of the Bible. The authors essentially say, "These things weren't done in a corner. There are hundreds of eyewitnesses. Here are some specific individuals. Ask them yourselves for further verification[37]."

---

[36] Cold-Case Christianity, Chapter 7, J. Warner Wallace

[37] Acts 26:26 NIV, paraphrased

The facts point to Jesus as God in the flesh. But can we trust a book that was written over 2,000 years ago? We'll explore that next.

CHAPTER 9

BATTING 1,000

Ted Williams of the Boston Red Sox is the last Major League baseball player to "bat .400". That means that he achieved a "hit" more than 4 out of every 10 times he got up to bat over the course of a baseball season. At just 23 years old, Ted Williams was batting .39955 heading into the baseball season's final day. The Red Sox were scheduled to play two games in Philadelphia against the Philadelphia Phillies. Legend has it that the Red Sox Manager, Joe Cronin, gave Williams the option to sit out the two games to protect his official batting average of .400. But Williams didn't want to hit .400 with an average that needed to be rounded up. He ended up playing and hitting safely in 6 out of his 8 at-bats, finishing the season with an average of .406. He made history.

So, just how difficult is it to "bat .400"? It hasn't been done in nearly 80 years. This all occurred back in 1941, and the achievement of batting .400 is still considered the standard of hitting excellence.[38]

Batting .400 over the course of a 162-game baseball season is an amazing accomplishment. But how about batting a perfect 1,000 over the course of 2,000+ years? That's what we're talking about when we examine the reliability of the Bible.

---

[38] Ted Williams - Wikipedia

Takeaway #3 is the Bible is the most studied and scrutinized text in history, and it's not close.

Put simply, if it could have been proven unreliable, it would have by now. If there were a series of false statements or contradictions that could falsify the Bible, it would have been done by now[39]. This is like having the best pitchers in the world spend their lifetimes trying to strike you out, and not being able to do it, ever. They study you; they accuse you of cheating, they scrutinize you every day for 2,000 years. Yet, you're still batting 1,000. This is made even more amazing because the Bible isn't even really just one book. It's a collection of 66 books written by 40 authors over the course of 1,500 years. There are books on history, philosophy, ethics, and theology, among other topics and yet, there is a common thread woven through all 66 books. They all point to one perfect person. **They all point to Jesus**[40]. We'll discuss that further in Chapter 12, but for our purposes now, let's focus on the New Testament portion of the Bible, which details the life and teachings of Jesus.

"Can we really trust a book that was written over 2,000 years ago?" On its face, it seems like a reasonable concern, but as I learned from Christian Apologist, Dr. William Lane Craig, there is an error within the question. The question assumes that we're worried about the gap in time between the events and today as if the events happened 2,000 years ago, and we're looking at fresh evidence today. That's not the case. What we're more concerned with is the gap in time between the events and the evidence. In other words, if the New Testament writings were reliable historical evidence about Jesus' life and resurrection when they were written, they don't somehow turn into bad evidence for those events just because time has gone by since they were written[41]. We have many reasons to believe that the New Testament writings are reliable[42]. Consider that:

The accounts were written early. As discussed in the previous chapter, the New Testament was written during the first century, well within the lifetimes of eyewitnesses to the events. That includes people who knew Jesus during his lifetime and those who witnessed Jesus after he rose from the dead. It also includes hostile eyewitnesses, who could have refuted any of the claims if they were known to be false.

There are multiple, independent accounts of the events. For example, there are four Gospels in the New Testament that detail the life and teachings of Jesus. These were written by either eyewitnesses or those who had second-hand testimony from eyewitnesses. These four gospels have gone through the most intense scrutiny imaginable and are considered to be totally reliable.

There are differences between the Gospels. The differences that critics have tried to use to discredit the Gospels are actually a piece of evidence that supports their reliability. If the Gospels had been identical, it would indicate that they could have been fabricated. Rather, there are enough differences in the secondary details that indicate these are independent and consistent accounts.

The writers were careful historians. For Instance, Luke, the writer of approximately ¼ of the New Testament, cites 32 countries, 54 cities, and 9 islands. His geographical references have been verified as 100% accurate (Case for Christ- cite). This is particularly impressive to me,

---

[41] Youtube: Can We Trust The Bible Written 2000 Years Ago? Dr. William Lane Craig

[42] These concepts can be found throughout the recommended book list.

someone who uses GPS to drive to places within a half-hour of where I grew up. But the point is that the supreme diligence the writers demonstrated in seemingly less important information indicates the supreme diligence they would apply to much more critical details of the accounts.

Archeology supports the accounts. The more we dig, the more support we gain for the New Testament accounts. Archeology has even verified passages that critics initially rejected because they appeared to contradict what we knew about geography. As archaeology supports the Bible, it can be crushing to other religions[43].

The accounts include embarrassing details. There are details included in the New Testament writings that would never be included if they were made up. Some of these details, make Jesus' closest followers look foolish, weak, scared, etc. For example; a made-up account of Jesus' resurrection would likely include one of Jesus' Apostles discovering the empty tomb. But the New Testament tells about how the Apostles deserted him and were in hiding because they feared for their lives. They didn't bravely go to the tomb. It was Mary Magdalen and a group of women who found the empty tomb. This is particularly telling; given that we're talking about the first century when the testimony of women was not even considered valid in the courts of law. This is not a detail that would be included unless it were true.

---

[43] The Case for Christ, Chapter 5, Lee Strobel

Non-Christian authors wrote about Jesus. 10+ non-Christian authors within 150 years of Jesus' life wrote about him[44].

Finally, the quantity of documents blows away any other document in history, so we know we're getting an accurate picture of what the documents said when they were written. Of course, with human scribes manually writing out copies, there are minor errors in individual manuscripts. Still, we can verify exactly what the original documents said based on the thousands of manuscripts available.

Takeaway #4 is that the New Testament documents were reliable historical evidence for Jesus' life and resurrection when they were written. They don't turn into bad evidence because time has gone by since they were written[45].

This leads us to a crossroads in our journey. Christianity, Judaism, and Islam cannot all be right about Jesus. Either Jesus is God in the flesh or He is not. CS Lewis famously destroyed any middle ground in his classic, Mere Christianity[46]:

"I am trying here to prevent anyone saying the really foolish thing that people often say about Him: I'm ready to accept Jesus as a great moral teacher, but I don't accept his claim to be God. That is the one thing we must not say. A man who was merely a man and said the sort of things Jesus said would not be a great moral teacher. He

---

[44] I Don't Have Enough Faith to be an Atheist, Chapter 9, Frank Turek and Norm Geisler

[45] Youtube: Can We Trust The Bible Written 2000 Years Ago? Dr. William Lane Craig

[46] Mere Christianity, Chapter 3, CS Lewis

would be either a lunatic—on a level with the man who says he is a poached egg—or else he would be the Devil of Hell. You must make your choice. Either this man was, and is, the Son of God, or else a madman or something worse. You can shut him up for a fool, you can spit at him and kill him as a demon or you can fall at his feet and call him Lord and God, but let us not come with any patronizing nonsense about his being a great human teacher. He has not left that open to us. He did not intend to. Now it seems to me obvious that He was neither a lunatic nor a fiend; and consequently, however strange or terrifying or unlikely it may seem, I have to accept the view that He was and is God".

Great moral teachers don't claim to BE God. Great moral teachers don't have the authority to forgive sins, nor do they perform miracles like giving sight to the blind. A decision must be made.

Takeaway #5 is that Jesus is either a liar, a lunatic, or Lord of all.

PART 3 REVIEW

"Here is a man who was born in an obscure village, the child of a peasant woman. He grew up in another village. He worked in a carpenter shop until He was thirty. Then for three years, He was an itinerant preacher. He never owned a home. He never wrote a book. He never held an office. He never had a family. He never went to college. He never put His foot inside a big city. He never traveled two hundred miles from the place He was born. He never did one of the things that usually accompany greatness. He had no credentials but Himself... While still a young man, the tide of popular opinion turned against him. His friends ran away. One of them denied him. He was turned over to His enemies. He went through the mockery of a trial. He was nailed upon a cross between two thieves. While He was dying His executioners gambled for the only piece of property He had on earth—His

> coat. When He was dead, He was laid in a borrowed grave through the pity of a friend. Nineteen long centuries have come and gone, and today He is a centerpiece of the human race and leader of the column of progress. I am far within the mark when I say that all the armies that ever marched, all the navies that were ever built, all the parliaments that ever sat and all the kings that ever reigned, put together, have not affected the life of man upon this earth as powerfully as that one solitary life."
> -Dr. James Allan Francis[47]

Let's review what we know.

1. Jesus' followers claimed he appeared to them after his execution even though they had every incentive to deny it. It is nonsensical to think that they would subject themselves to persecution, interrogation, torture, and death for something they knew to be a lie.
2. Over the course of decades of interrogation, not one of the hundreds of eyewitnesses ever recanted their testimony about Jesus rising from the dead. The resurrection is neither a conspiracy theory nor a myth[48].
3. The Bible, which tells us that Jesus is God in the flesh, is the most studied and scrutinized text in history, and it's not close[49].
4. The New Testament documents were reliable historical evidence for Jesus' life and resurrection when they were written. They don't turn into bad evidence because time has gone by since they were written[50].

---

[47] One Solitary Life, Dr. James Allan Francis

[48] Cold-Case Christianity, Chapter 7, J. Warner Wallace

[49] Youtube: Ravi Zacharias Q&A How Do We Know the Bible is True?

[50] Youtube: Can We Trust The Bible Written 2000 Years Ago? Dr. William Lane Craig

5. Jesus is either a liar, a lunatic, or Lord of all[51].

Bottom Line #2: Jesus Christ of Nazareth is the single most influential person in history. Two thousand plus years after being executed in the most shameful way imaginable, He is revered by followers on every continent of our planet. He is God in the flesh. The God of the Bible is the one true God.

---

[51] Mere Christianity, Chapter 3, CS Lewis

PART 4
GOD'S WORD

CHAPTER 10

HE'S BEEN THERE ALL ALONG

> *"The word of God is active and alive, sharper than any double-edged sword"* Hebrews 4:12

Christianity isn't a blind faith that we agree to be true just because we want it to be. What we've done to get to this point in our study is simply follow the evidence where it leads. We examined scientific and philosophical evidence to prove that some God or gods exist. We then ruled out the belief systems that are not consistent with God's characteristics. This confirmed that there is <u>one</u> Creator, God who exists independent of the universe (monotheism). Finally, we examined the paramount difference between the three major monotheistic religions: Jesus Christ. We examined the reliability of the Bible, specifically the portions that describe Jesus' life and teachings. This is not a new exercise since the Bible is by far the most scrutinized text in history. It was and is still "batting 1,000." Accordingly, the life, death, and resurrection of Jesus proves that the God of the Bible is the one true God. This does not mean that all other religions are devoid of truth or goodness. But it does mean that any teaching that contradicts the Bible is false.

We know that to be true because Jesus said so. He taught that the Old Testament, the portion of the Bible which was written before his earthly lifetime, is the inerrant Word of God. Inerrant means incapable of being wrong. This makes for a very straightforward way to adjudicate issues using the Bible. God in the flesh taught that the Bible is incapable of being wrong. Therefore, if what I believe contradicts the Bible, then my belief is wrong. Or if I believe that there is an error in the Bible, I am in error. Andy Stanley, Founding Pastor of North Point Community Church in Alpharetta, GA, conveys this sentiment beautifully[52]:

"My high school science teacher told me that much of Genesis is false. But since my high school teacher did not prove he was God by rising from the dead, I'm going to believe Jesus instead."

It should also be noted that Jesus taught that the New Testament, the portion of the Bible written after his (earthly) lifetime, would come through His apostles. Specifically, that the Apostles would be inspired and aided by the Holy Spirit in this writing.

Bottom Line #3 is that the Bible truly is the inerrant word of God.

The sacred writings of the Bible are called scriptures. Given that the starting point of our study was whether there was any God at all, I deliberately focused on evidence outside of the Bible to prove that there is one Creator God who exists independent of the universe. Now that we have followed the evidence to this point, it's important to understand that the Word of God has been there all along.

Evidence, whether scientific, philosophical, moral, or otherwise, is only valid if it's in line with God's Word. By now,

---

[52] Andy Stanley, Pastor of North Point Community Church in Alpharetta, GA

you know what's coming: there's a spreadsheet for that. This will show you that, while we arrived at these takeaways using information outside of the Bible, each one of them is directly in line with what the Bible says.

TAKEAWAY	GOD'S WORD[53]
God caused the universe to explode into being, out of nothing.	Genesis 1:1- In the beginning God created the heavens and the earth.
God tuned up the universe to allow life.	Jeremiah 51:15- It is he who made the earth by his power, who established the world by his wisdom, and by his understanding stretched out the heavens.
God designed D.N.A., the unimaginably complex instruction book for life.	Hebrews 3:4- For every house is built by someone but the builder of all things is God.
Microevolution exists. Macroevolution appears false because it is.	Genesis 1:27- So God created mankind in his own image, in the image of God he created them; male and female he created them.
Science is a process we use to learn about the universe God created.	Genesis 1:31- God saw all that he had made, and it was very good. And there was evening, and there was morning-- the sixth day Thus the heavens and earth were completed in all their vast array.

---

[53] NIV

Moral laws are like the laws of mathematics. People do not invent them, yet they apply to everyone. They would be true even if there were no one on the planet.	Colossians 1:16- For in him all things were created: things in heaven and on earth, visible and invisible, whether thrones or powers or rulers or authorities; all things have been created through him and for him.
Anytime you disagree with someone else's moral values, you're acknowledging that there is an unchanging standard outside of humanity that applies to everyone.	Romans 1:20- For since the creation of the world God's invisible qualities—his eternal power and divine nature—have been clearly seen, being understood from what has been made, so that people are without excuse.
Just like the disagreement on time required a standard outside of watches, morality requires a standard outside of human opinion. That measuring stick is called God. Society is not outside of human opinion.	Acts 5:29- Peter and the other apostles replied: "We must obey God rather than human beings..."
Animals have no moral obligation to one another. Humans do.	Romans 2:15- They show that the requirements of the law are written on their hearts, their consciences also bearing witness, and their thoughts sometimes accusing them and at other times even defending them.
The existence of basic human rights assumes the	Psalm 139:14- I praise you because I was fearfully and wonderfully made; your works

existence of a Creator, God.	are wonderful, I know that full well.

When we follow this evidence that is in line with God's word, it allows us to reach conclusions that are in line with God's word.

BOTTOM LINE	GOD'S WORD[54]
The evidence proves that God exists	Isaiah 44:6- "This is what the Lord says—Israel's King and Redeemer, the Lord Almighty: I am the first and I am the last; apart from me there is no God..."
Jesus Christ of Nazareth is God in the flesh. The God of the Bible is the one true God.	Hebrews 1:3- The Son is the radiance of God's glory and the exact representation of his being, sustaining all things by his powerful word.
The Bible truly is the inerrant word of God.	2 Timothy 3:16- All scripture is God-breathed and is useful for teaching, rebuking, correcting and training in righteousness, so that the servant of God may be thoroughly equipped for every good work.

Proper science, philosophy, and logic line up with the Bible because, like everything else in the universe, science, philosophy and logic were created by God. We have found the truth that unlocks everything else in this life! Let's do some unlocking together, friend.

---

[54] NIV

PART 5
THE GOOD NEWS

CHAPTER 11

THE WEDDING CAKE WORLDVIEW

"So we just go and get to try all different types of cake?" I was waiting for some sort of "catch" because the idea of a wedding cake tasting session sounded too good to be true. Granted, the average wedding cake costs around $500, so there is a price to pay, but how often in life is it your obligation as a good husband to take one for the team and try all different types of cake? The tasting did not disappoint, and neither did the vanilla wedding cake with raspberry filling that we ultimately chose.

When people think of weddings, the cake is often one of the first things that comes to mind. Even guests who don't really want to be attending the wedding are hoping there is a good cake as a silver lining. This has been going on since the days of the Roman Empire when husbands would crumble a cake of wheat or barley over the bride's head to symbolize fertility and bring good fortune to the couple[55]. Today, these cakes are often multi-tiered works of art displayed as a centerpiece at the wedding reception. The newlyweds traditionally cut the cake together and take turns feeding a bite to their spouse. There is that moment of suspense for the guests as they wait to see if there will be a "cake smash" resulting in the newlyweds'

---

[55] Wedding cake - Wikipedia

faces being covered in frosting. The top of the cake is then set aside to be saved and eaten by the newlyweds on their first anniversary.

For all of the well-known things about wedding cakes, I learned something through the process of buying one that absolutely shocked me. And no, it wasn't just the price. **I had no idea that oftentimes the wedding cake on display is fake.** The top tier that the newlyweds cut is actual cake, but the rest of the tiers are Styrofoam "dummies" covered in frosting. There are then sheet cakes back in the kitchen that are cut up and served to the guests. The fake cake is less expensive and so can be used as a cost-saving measure for the newlyweds. I had no idea!

I tell you all of this because many people suffer from a **Wedding Cake Worldview**. It comes in various forms but can generally be summed up as the belief that "Kindness is all that matters." It's the idea that all religious ideas are equally true, and that in the end life is just about being kind to one another. That sounds great, doesn't it? Here's the thing. The wedding cake appears magnificent on the surface, but underneath the frosting, it's basically hollow. It's Styrofoam. It's not real. "Kindness is all that matters" also sounds great on the surface, but it's hollow. It's shallow. It's not real.

The wedding cake has a small portion of real cake to it, the top tier that the newlyweds cut. Similarly, "Kindness is all that matters" has a small portion of truth to it. Yes, it's true that being kind matters. But it's not all that matters. Now don't misunderstand. Of course, the Christian belief encompasses "kindness." Jesus took human ethics to the highest plain known to man. For instance, he taught, *"You have heard that it was said, 'Love your neighbor and hate your enemies.' But I tell you, love your enemies and pray for those who persecute you, that you may be children of your Father in heaven.*[56]*"*

---

[56] Matthew 5:43 NIV

Unfortunately, many don't even realize that the Wedding Cake Worldview is fake. We just keep sloshing frosting onto that Styrofoam to make it taste better. The frosting could be money, sex, accomplishments, likes, fame; you name it. The pleasures of the world can taste sweet at the moment, but ultimately if you're eating that Styrofoam layer, you'll never be nourished, never be satisfied and if you eat it for too long, you'll be sick. Think about it; if the pleasures of the world were all that mattered, then every rich and famous person should be eternally happy. And yet, we know that's not the case.

Just as using the Styrofoam "dummies" means the cake is cheaper and easier to make, it's cheaper and easier to dabble in spiritual pursuits than it is to commit. We're choking down Styrofoam when we attempt to acknowledge the one true God of the Bible but also dabble in a smorgasbord of beliefs like nature worship, yoga, psychics, meditation, horoscopes, etc. In a world where "kindness is all that matters," religion is more of a preference than a matter of ultimate truth.

But the truth is that we long for something real, for something deeper; we long for answers to the questions that really matter, like:

- -How did I get here?
- -Is there a purpose for my life?
- -Is this "it," or is there an eternal afterlife?

> ***"Kindness is all that matters"*** *answers none of this. The Good News of Jesus Christ answers all of this.*

We've discovered the truth that unlocks all of this! We want the real deal. We want the good stuff. It's time to "taste and see that the Lord is good[57]." Let's explore the Gospel (Good News) of Jesus Christ:

Have you had a sinless day yet? A day where every thought, feeling, and action of yours were perfectly moral and perfectly just? I haven't yet, and as of 8:15 AM, I can tell you that today is not that day. I've already gotten frustrated with my kids and yelled at them for interrupting my thought process while trying to write. I know I'm not perfect, and I'm going to bet that you know you're not perfect either. The truth is that we all know that there isn't a person walking this earth who is perfect.

That's an issue. That's an issue because we've already established that our entire universe, including you and I, were created by a perfect God. Humans are God's masterpiece; the only beings in creation that were made in his image. So if God is perfect and we are made in His image, then we should be perfect too, right? We were. But we blew it. You probably know the story. The first humans, Adam and Eve, were placed in a perfect paradise called the Garden of Eden. They were in a perfect relationship with their Creator, God. God told them that they could eat from any tree except the tree of knowledge of good and evil. Adam and Eve rebelled against God, disobeyed Him, and ate from the tree (you had one job, guys!). Because of this Original Sin, all humans have inherited a sinful nature, and we all choose to sin. That explains why you never have and never will know someone perfect.

So what does this mean for us? Our purpose is to live in an eternal, perfect relationship with our God. That's how God designed it. But the Bible tells us that the wages of sin is death. In other words, how could we be in a perfect relationship with our Creator when we ourselves are no longer perfect? He can't tolerate evil.

---

[57] Psalm 34:8 NIV

Deep down, we yearn for that relationship with our Creator, and so our natural reaction is to try and fix it. Maybe if we do enough good deeds, or pray enough, or meditate enough, we'll get back to perfection. Wrong. Even our good deeds end up being an extension of our selfishness and a lifetime of good deeds doesn't somehow erase all of the bad stuff we've done. Maybe if I get enough money, or accolades, or likes, or fame, I'll get back to perfection. Wrong. We know that's just frosting covering up a hollow inside. It will never nourish us. The reality is that we couldn't fix it then, and we'll never be able to fix it. We are all sinners, and therefore we deserve death.

Yikes. That's pretty depressing. There's a reason why this is called THE GOOD NEWS of Jesus Christ!

We know God is perfectly moral, and so justice must be done. But God is also perfect love. So how can God serve perfect justice and also love us, his children, perfectly? Someone without sin had to willingly take our place to pay the cost for our sins. Since the only one who is perfect is God, it had to be Him.

God sent Himself as Jesus, God in the flesh, to pay the cost for us. His death functions as payment for our sins. **All we need to do is to accept Jesus Christ as our Lord and Savior, and we are free**. We are pardoned. We are no longer slaves to fear. God forgives our sins, and we return to perfect unity with Him. The Bible says that "as far as the East is from the West, so far has he removed our transgressions from us." Everything we've ever done wrong is forgiven and removed from us.

This is the Gospel. This is the Good News. No amount of good deeds can put us back into right relationship with God. But Jesus took our place and did it for us. He took our sins, took our shame, took our guilt on that cross. If we'll just put our faith in Jesus, and I'll explain exactly how you can do that later in this book, we are free indeed!

PART 6

I DON'T WANT IT TO SEEM LIKE I'M QUESTIONING, BUT...

> *Now Thomas (also known as Didymus), one of the Twelve, was not with the disciples when Jesus came. So the other disciples told him, "We have seen the Lord!". But he said to them, "Unless I see the nail marks in his hands and put my finger where the nails were, and my put hand into his side, I will not believe." A week later his disciples were in the house again, and Thomas was with them. Though the doors were locked, Jesus came and stood among them and said, "Peace be with you!" Then he said to Thomas, "Put your finger here, see my hands. Reach out your hand and put it into my side. Stop doubting and believe." Thomas said to him, "My Lord and my God!". Then Jesus told him, "Because you have seen me, you have believed; blessed are those who have not seen and believed[58]."*

Thomas, one of Jesus' twelve closest followers, had doubts. After Jesus was crucified and appeared to the other Apostles, Thomas declared he wouldn't believe unless he saw Jesus for himself and even put his hands in Jesus' wounds. You've heard the term "Doubting Tom" before, right? This is where it comes from. In any sense, this is a man who spent years with Jesus, hearing His teachings and witnessing His miracles. Yet, he had questions and doubts.

And you somehow feel guilty about having doubts over 2,000 years later?

It's OK to have questions. We are wise to treat our faith like it's a muscle and when we don't use our muscles, they waste away but when we work them and put them through resistance, they grow stronger. When you believe in the one true God, you have truth on your side. Your faith will only be strengthened as you work through questions and understand *why* you believe.

I've been asked questions about Christianity with qualifiers like "I don't want to seem like I'm doubting, but... what about XYZ?"

---

[58] John 20:24 NIV

Now that we've established it's OK to ask, let's pump some spiritual iron and build our faith!

CHAPTER 12

FAQ's

1. What does it mean to be "born again"?

My wife and I recently started watching a sitcom called "The Good Place." The show's setting is a heaven-like afterlife that only the most moral people on earth can get into. Admission to the "good place" is determined by a sort of cosmic in-house accounting firm. Every action a person takes on earth has a point total attached to it. Unbeknownst to the people while they are alive, their good deeds earn them points, and their bad deeds lose them points. Their life's actions add up to a score, and that score determines whether or not they are eligible for "The Good Place." If their score doesn't make the cut, they're sent down to "The Bad Place" to be tortured for eternity. Life on earth is basically boiled down to a standardized test.

The show explores some interesting philosophical and moral issues, but what stuck out to me is that this concept of the cosmic accounting firm isn't too far off from some actual Wedding Cake Worldviews. Essentially, do enough good deeds to overshadow your bad ones and hope you make the cut. But as we know from the Gospel, we're created by a perfect God, and He serves perfect justice. Since we are all sinners, none of us would "qualify" for "The Good Place" on our own. The only way we can be saved is by accepting the free gift from God that Jesus paid for by dying on the cross. To explore this, let's move out of the world of fantasy and back to first-century Jerusalem.

Now there was a Pharisee (religious leader), a man named Nicodemus who was a member of the Jewish ruling council. He came to Jesus at night and said, "Rabbi, we know that you are a teacher who has come from God. For no one could perform the signs you are doing if God were not with him. Jesus replied, **"Very truly I tell you, no one can see the kingdom of God unless they are born again."** *"How can someone be born when they are old?" Nicodemus asked. "Surely they cannot enter a second time into their mother's womb to be born[59]!"*

The scripture goes on to explain that we are spiritually "born again" when we decide to believe in Jesus as our Lord and Savior. What does a Savior do? They save you when you can't save yourself. When Jesus began his work during this earthly life, His message was *"The time has come. The kingdom of God has come near. Repent and believe the good news[60]!"*. To repent means to turn, to change and the bottom line of what He's saying is to turn away from the route you're going and believe the Good News instead.

To absorb the Good News, you must understand you can't earn your way into that perfect relationship with God. If we could ever do it ourselves, then Jesus suffering and dying on the cross for us would have been for nothing. The only way we can be born again spiritually is by putting our trust in Jesus and by accepting that gift.

This plays itself out in a common misperception of what it means to be a Christian. Namely, that Christians change their behavior because they're trying to be saved. The truth is that Christians don't try to clean up their act and live according to the Bible *so that* they can be saved; Christians try to clean up their act and live according to the Bible **because** they've been saved. It's a one-time event that happens when you put your

---

[59] John 3:1-3 NIV emphasis added

[60] Mark 1:15 NIV

trust in Jesus. The Bible explains it like this: "*I will give you a new heart and put a new spirit in you; I will remove from you your heart of stone and give you a heart of flesh.*" It's not about trying to earn something when they turn away from sins; they're acting differently because spiritually they've been born again. I'll explain how to do this later in this book.

2. Are Jesus and God the same? What about the Holy Spirit?

The short answer is yes and no. What we are talking about is what's known as the trinity. We've concluded that the God of the Bible is the one true God and that the Bible is the inerrant word of God. So to go even deeper and learn more about God, we look to the Bible. The Bible tells us this:

There is only one God, eternally existent in three distinct co-equal persons: Father, Son, and Holy Spirit.

That's a mouth full so let's break it down.

1. **There is only one God**. Therefore, there are NOT three Gods. We already determined that polytheism, the idea that there is more than one God, is false. There is only one Creator; God, who exists independent of the universe.
2. **The one true God exists as three distinct persons**. Therefore, Jesus is distinct from the Father and the Holy Spirit. Likewise, the Father is distinct from Jesus and The Holy Spirit, and The Holy Spirit is distinct from Jesus and the Father.
3. **The one true God is eternally existent**. A common question from skeptics says, "If the God of the Bible created the universe, then who created God? The answer is no one! If someone had created the God of the Bible, that someone would actually be God. Or, if someone had created the God that created the God of the Bible, *that* someone would actually be God. Do you see how this could go on forever? At some point, there

must be a first cause. The God of the Bible is that first cause.
4. **The three distinct persons exist as co-equals.** Because Jesus is known as the Son of God, there is a common misunderstanding that He was created by God the Father. This is false. The Son is a role, just as the Father and the Holy Spirit are both roles. These three roles are distinct from one another, yet exist co-equally. The Bible teaches us that all three persons of the trinity are eternal.

So, where human beings are one being who exists as one person, God is one being who exists as three persons. This is difficult for us to compute because we don't know anyone like that on Earth. Of course we don't. God told us we wouldn't. *"I am God, and there is no other, I am God, and there is none like me[61]."* Most people can barely understand the opposite sex. It shouldn't be a shocker that you are unable to fully grasp an infinite God. The evidence confirms that God exists, the Bible reveals more about him, but there is a limit to human knowledge about God. Again, He told us it would be so. *Great is the Lord, and highly to be praised, and his greatness is unsearchable[62].* Outside of the Bible, we can see God's glory when we look into the eyes of our children, when we look out into the ocean or when we look up to the stars. When you consider that He created all of that from nothing, it's a reminder that the God of the Bible is far more glorious than we can even comprehend. All we can do is praise His mighty name.

A final piece of logic that helps explain the trinity is that God is love. Pastor Timothy Keller explains this brilliantly in his New York Times bestseller "The Reason for God." Essentially, when

---

[61] Isaiah 46:9 NIV

[62] Psalm 145 NKJV

people say that God is love, they usually mean that love is important or that God encourages us to love others. But for Christians, we actually mean that God **IS** love. Within the one being of God, the three persons of the trinity eternally love one another, glorify one another, adore one another. Love is something that one person feels for another, so if God were just one person, love would not have existed until He began creating other beings. Because all three parts of the trinity have existed for eternity, God's very essence is eternal love. God literally is love[63].

3. What does it mean that Jesus is "the Messiah"?

God promised the nation of Israel that He would deliver a Savior, a righteous High Priest and King of kings who would sit on the throne forever[64]. He is referred to as the Messiah, or "Anointed One," which refers to the Hebrew ritual act of anointing those with oil to designate a priestly or royal position. Over the course of hundreds of years, God delivered messages about this Messiah using prophets. God calls these Prophets to this role, and He essentially speaks through them to deliver various messages. The prophecies about the Messiah are recorded in the Old Testament of the Bible, the portion written before Jesus' earthly lifetime. The result is amazing. This Old Testament, a collection of 39 books by 35 authors written over the course of 1,000+ years, all point to one person, one perfect person; The Messiah. There were 60 major Old Testament Prophecies about the Messiah written more than 400 years before Jesus was born. We can use these prophecies to determine whether Jesus meets the job description.

---

[63] The Reason for God, Chapter 14, Pastor Timothy Keller

[64] 77 FAQs About God and the Bible, Chapter 42, John McDowell and Sean McDowell

Job Title: Messiah[65]

Job Description: High Priest, King of Kings, Savior of the whole world

OLD TESTAMENT PROPHECY[66]	NECESSARY QUALIFICATIONS
NIV	NIV
Micah 5:2 — "The Coming Messiah" But you, Bethlehem, Though you are small among the clans of Judah, out of you shall come for me one who will be ruler over Israel, whose origins are from old, from ancient times.	Must be born in a tiny town called Bethlehem
Isaiah 35:5- Then will the eyes of the blind be opened and the ears of the deaf unstopped, then the lame will leap like a deer and the mute tongue shout for joy.	Must be a miracle worker
Isaiah 53:12- He poured out his life unto death and was numbered with the transgressors.	Must be executed among sinners
Isaiah 53:12- He bore the sin of many and made intercession for the transgressors.	Must pray for his persecutors
Psalm 22:16- Dogs surround me, a pack of villains encircles me; they pierce my hands and my feet	Must have hands and feet pierced

---

[65] Charts based on info from 77 FAQ's about God and the Bible, Josh McDowell and Sean McDowell

[66] NIV

Psalm 110:1- **The Lord says to my Lord, sit at my right hand until I make your enemies a footstool for your feet**	Must be raised from the dead, go up to heaven and be seated at the right hand of the Father

Do we know any eligible candidates? To compile Jesus' resume, we'll reference the New Testament of the Bible, the portion written after the earthly life of Jesus.

Old Testament Prophecy[67]	**Qualification**	**Jesus' Resume**[68]
Isaiah 7:14- Therefore the Lord himself will give you a sign: The virgin will conceive and give birth to a son, and will call him Immanuel (God with us)	Must be born of a virgin	Luke 1:31- You will conceive and give birth to a Son, and you are to call him Jesus... Then Mary said to the angel, How can this be, since I am a virgin? The angel answered, "The Holy Spirit will come on you, and the power of the most High will overshadow you. So the holy one to be born will be called the Son of God.
Micah 5:1 — "The Coming Messiah" But you, Bethlehem, Though you are little among the thousands of Judah, Yet out of you shall come forth to Me, The One to be Ruler in Israel, Whose going forth are from of old, From Everlasting	Must be born in a tiny town called Bethlehem	Matthew 2:1- After Jesus was born in Bethlehem in Judea, during the time of King Herod, Magi from the east came to Jerusalem 2and asked, "Where is the one who has been born king of the Jews? We saw his star when it rose and have come to worship him.

---

[67] NIV

[68] NIV

Isaiah 35:5- Then will the eyes of the blind be opened and the ears of the deaf unstopped, then the lame will leap like a deer and the mute tongue shout for joy.	Must be a miracle worker	**Matthew 9:35**- Jesus went through all the towns and villages, teaching in their synagogues, proclaiming the good news of the kingdom and healing every disease and sickness.
Isaiah 53:12- He poured out his life unto death and was numbered with the transgressors.	Must be executed among sinners	**Matthew 27:38**- Two rebels were crucified with him, one on his right and one on his left.
Isaiah 53:12- He bore the sin of many and made intercession for the transgressors.	Must pray for his persecutors	**Luke 23:34**- Jesus said, Father, forgive them, for they do not know what they are doing.
Psalm 22:16- Dogs surround me, a pack of villains encircles me, they pierce my hands and my feet	Must have hands and feet pierced	**Luke 23:33**- when they came to the place called the Skull, they crucified him there, along with the criminals, one on his right, the other on his left.
Psalm 110:1- The Lord says to my Lord, sit at my right hand until I make your enemies a footstool for your feet	Must be raised from the dead, go up to heaven and be sated at the right hand of the Father	**Acts 2:32**- God has raised this Jesus to life and we are all witnesses of it. Exalted to the right hand of God, he has received from the Father the promised Holy Spirit and has poured out what you now see and hear.

Speaking about the Old Testament, Jesus said, *"Do not think that I have come to abolish the Law or the Prophets; I have not come to abolish them but to **fulfill** them[69],"* and indeed he did. In Lee Strobel's book "Case for Christ," he explains that one person's

---

[69] Matthew 5:17 NIV

probability of fulfilling just eight prophecies is 1 in 100 million billion. What does that number look like? It's the odds that you would choose a specific silver dollar if the entire state of Texas were covered in silver dollars two feet deep and you were blindfolded. That's the odds to fulfill 8 prophecies in a lifetime. Jesus fulfilled 29 prophecies in one day![70] By the way, do you know the Greek translation for Messiah? It's **Christ**. As in Jesus Christ of Nazareth. Jesus is the Messiah.

4. How could a loving God allow so much pain and suffering in the world?

The evidence for God is abundant. It's not so much a lack of evidence as it is anger at God that causes many to turn away from Him. Awful, painful things happen in this world, and we wonder, "If God really is good and all-powerful, why would He let this happen? He must either not be all good or not be all-powerful." To some extent, I think we've all been there. We've been through the moral law argument that proves God is the ultimate measuring stick of what's right and wrong. So how do we reconcile all of this pain and suffering with an all-loving and all-powerful God? Two words: *Free Will*. Follow me on this.

God's very essence, the eternal Trinity, is love. God is love. We were created in the image of God, and therefore, are designed to love God and love people. Therein lies the rub. **Love requires free will**. The Creator of the universe could have designed us to be robots who behaved perfectly, but you can't force love. If it were forced, it wouldn't be true love. Love must be entered into voluntarily. So God gave us free will that we would have the capacity to love, and so we do. The tradeoff that comes with this capacity to love is that free will also give us the capacity to sin. And as we know, every person has inherited a sinful nature from Adam and Eve. We are all sinners, and it's this sin that causes pain and suffering on the planet. It's this sin that

---

[70] 77 FAQs About God and the Bible, Chapter 42, John McDowell and Sean McDowell

separated us from God and necessitated Jesus to die on the cross to fix it[71].

When considering this problem of pain, we must also remember that God takes what seems to be meant for our harm and turns it for our good. The Bible tells us to *"Consider it pure joy, my brothers and sisters, whenever you face trials of many kinds, because you know that the testing of your faith produces perseverance. Let perseverance finish its work so that you may be mature and complete, not lacking anything.*[72]" Consider it pure joy when I have a problem? Easier said than done, but we're not on earth just to enjoy pleasure for a short time. We're having our character developed in preparation for an eternity with God in glory. If you're a parent you know that as much as you hate to see your kids in pain, you're willing to let them go through some trials to grow. They don't understand it at the moment but you, as a parent, see the bigger picture for them. So it is with our heavenly Father. He uses pain to develop our character and to draw us closer to him. C.S. Lewis explained it like this: "Pain insists upon being attended to. God whispers to us in our pleasures, speaks in our consciences, but shouts in our pains. It is his megaphone to rouse a deaf world.[73]" There is nothing like pain to get our undivided attention, especially when we start falling into that trap that makes us think we are in full control of our lives. Pain reminds us that we're not meant to do it all on our own and that we need God.

5. How could a loving God send someone to hell?

In air travel, the 1 in 60 rule states that if a pilot is 1 degree off course, every 60 miles of flight will cause the plane to miss its

---

[71] YouTube: Cross Examined, How To Better Approach The Subject Of Hell, Frank Turek

[72] James 1:2 NIV

[73] The Problem of Pain, CS Lewis

target location by 1 mile[74]. So for a quick 60-mile flight, one degree off course sends you just a mile away from your destination. Not too bad. But the longer you fly off course, the further you end up from your destination. If a plane flew the ~3,000 miles across the country at just 1 percent off course, it would end up approximately 50 miles away from its destination. Not ideal.

We were created to "fly" in perfect relationship with God forever, but the sinful nature that we inherited from Adam and Eve knocked us off course. The more we sin, the further off course we get. When we talk about hell we're talking about a natural continuation of the flight path we choose in this life. Hell is the absence of God in the afterlife[75]. So the more we sin, the further off course we get, and ultimately the further from God we land in our final destination.

But God loves us too much to just let us go. We could adjust our flight path on our own, but we could never correct our course fully to get to our proper destination. What Jesus did on the cross was, allow us to fix our flight path instantly. No matter how far off course we've gone, our flight path can be radically changed.

So God is like the air traffic controller, offering us these new coordinates throughout our lives. He delivers the gospel (Good News) in countless ways—through friends, family, missionaries, the church, the Bible, technology like TV/podcasts/apps, dreams, visions and more. But here's the thing: we must give up our own flight path in order to accept these coordinates. It requires us to say "I can't do it on my own. I put my trust in you, Jesus. I'm taking your path, not my own."

---

[74] 1 in 60 rule - Wikipedia

[75] YouTube: Cross Examined, How To Better Approach The Subject Of Hell, Frank Turek

So you see, it's not God who sends anyone to hell. The air traffic controller sends us correct coordinates throughout our lives if we'll just turn off of our own path (repent) and take His (believe the Good News). But He loves us too much to force us to be with him. If we spend our entire lives ignoring and avoiding His coordinates, He allows us to continue on our way, and lets us choose our destination.

6. Why doesn't the Bible talk about dinosaurs?

The question of dinosaurs in the Bible is a part of a broader discussion, an in-house debate of sorts amongst Christians about how old the Earth is. I refer to it as "in-house" because, in Part 1, we already dismantled the idea that the universe is eternal or somehow came to be without God. This isn't a debate about whether God created the universe; it's a debate as to *when* God created the universe.

Those in the "Young Earth" camp generally believe that the Earth was created within the last 10,000 years, where those in the "Old Earth" camp believe that the Earth is more like 13.8 billion years old. It reflects varying interpretations of the book of Genesis in the Bible, which tells the story of creation. Genesis describes creation occurring over six days, with God resting on the seventh day. But there is debate as to whether the days are specifically referring to 24-hour periods or if the term "day" is being used to describe something more like an era. Think about it; we use the term "day" in plenty of ways other than the 24-hour meaning. If someone is going to have "their day in court," that could mean just one day, but it could also be describing a trial that lasts longer. Or if we say, "back in my day, kids played outside instead of sitting on iPad's all-day," we clearly aren't talking about one 24-hour period. There is also the issue that the first "day" doesn't occur until the third line in the Bible after it's already been declared that "In the beginning God created the heavens and Earth.[76]"

There's nothing wrong with working through these issues, but let's not bury the lead. Whether it was thousands, millions, or billions of years ago, the God of the Bible is the Creator of the universe. I reiterate this because the age of the universe is sometimes used to support a no-God worldview. But the great irony is that the no-God worldview has no scientific leg to stand on. Ken Ham, CEO of Answers in Genesis, sums it up when he says that "In order to get people to believe in an impossible process (macroevolution), you have to get people to believe in an incomprehensible amount of time[77]." In other words, if the no-God explanation doesn't make sense now, just state that it occurred millions and millions of years ago. But we know that the universe had a cause, the universe is tuned up to support life, instructions (DNA) require intelligence, and macroevolution has never been observed. The age of the universe changes none of that. So while it's an in-house debate as to when God created the universe, the evidence is rock solid *that* God created the universe. Remember, science says absolutely nothing. Scientists do.

It's that background that impacts the varying views of where dinosaurs fit in history. For an "Old Earther," the dinosaurs could have existed and been killed off by a meteor hitting the Earth 50+ million years ago. Where a "Young Earther" would, of course, have the dinosaurs created within the past 10,000 or so years and having existed with humans for a time.

This all leads to the question: why doesn't the Bible talk about dinosaurs? I've been asked this, pondered it, read up on it, and found that the best explanation is hidden in plain sight. **The Bible doesn't talk about dinosaurs because the Bible isn't a**

---

[76] YouTube: Cross Examined, How Old Is The Universe, Frank Turek

[77] YouTube: Six Thousand Years with Ken Ham

book about dinosaurs. The lightbulb flicked on for me when Dr. Frank Turek explained it[78]. The Bible is a collection of books, all of which point toward one perfect life: Jesus. This collection of books prepares us to be born again and saved by Jesus. Why would we expect it to delve into the topic of dinosaurs? Some of the creatures mentioned sound like a dinosaur, though it may be better translated as a crocodile. For instance, a "Leviathan" is described in the book of Job as having rows of shields on its back, fearsome teeth, etc. The term dinosaur (terrible lizard) wasn't even coined until 1841.

The bottom line is that the Bible is simply not a book about dinosaurs. For more information on that topic, I can recommend some gems from my son's bookshelf such as "Little Kids First BIG Book of Dinosaurs," "Dino Baseball," or "Never Ask a Dinosaur to Dinner."

7. Why doesn't God just reveal himself, so we have no doubt He exists?

I've wrestled with this one. Wouldn't it be easier if God just appeared to everyone and destroyed any doubt about His existence? I used to think so, but now I'm not so sure. For one, the Bible tells us that our perfect creator God is too glorious for us to even gaze upon. God told Moses, *"you cannot see my face, for no one may see me and live.[79]"* This makes sense to me. We stand in awe when we look at natural wonders like the Grand Canyon or the solar system. They are amazing to behold, and yet our God literally created them from nothing. How much more infinitely glorious must the Creator of the universe be!

But what about Jesus? The Bible tells us he is *"the radiance of God's glory and the exact representation of his being"*[80]. He took on

---

[78] YouTube: Cross Examined, What about the Dinosaurs? Frank Turek

[79] Exodus 33:20 NIV

[80] Hebrews 1:3 NIV

human form and revealed Himself to us before, so couldn't He do it again? It seems to me that, of course He could; He's God. So that leaves us in a position where we have no choice but to do the very things he wants us to: *trust Him and seek Him.* God tells us through His word that *"I love those who love me, and those who seek me diligently find me*[81]*."*

The necessity to seek God puts us in a position to build a loving relationship with Him. Think about the difference between: (1) a kid who works hard, scrapes and claws her way to saving money, saves up, and buys a car or (2) a trust fund kid whose parents pay for her to rent a car while on vacation. Aren't those cars most likely going to be treated completely differently from one another?

The opportunity to seek God is the adventure of a lifetime and if you seek Him, He will make himself known. He reveals Himself to us in all different ways, and we've all had experiences in our own lives or in someone we know where we say "that could only be God." Tonight my family and I will attend a special annual Thanksgiving Service at our church. Not one person has a magic lamp or an on-demand button to "make" God appear, but hundreds will share quick stories about what God has done for them over the past year.

If you want to know Him, seek Him out.

"Ask, and it will be given to you; seek, and you will find; knock, and it will be opened to you. For everyone who asks receives, and the one who seeks finds, and to the one who knocks it will be opened[82]*".*

8. Isn't it arrogant to think that Jesus is the only way?

One common objection to Christianity is that it seems arrogant or narrow-minded to believe that Jesus is the only way to be saved and put back into a perfect relationship with God. This

---

[81] Proverbs 8:7 NIV

[82] Matthew 7:7-8 NIV

criticism underscores the fact that it is much easier to subscribe to a Wedding Cake Worldview than to commit to Christianity. You will ruffle far fewer feathers if you believe that all religions are equally valid and there are many ways to get to heaven. But here's the thing; Christians didn't declare that Jesus was the only way. Jesus himself did.

Jesus answered, "I am the way and the truth and the life. No one comes to the Father except through me."[83]

God in the flesh has declared it on His own authority, so Christians believe it even though in many circles, it could make their lives easier to just go with the flow. **It's not arrogant to believe that Jesus is the only way.** *It's obedient.*

It's also important to point out that an objection like this has nothing to do with whether or not Jesus is actually the only way to God. Jesus is either God in the flesh, or He's not. A believer being arrogant or narrow-minded doesn't change that truth. Apply this concept to a current event. The Covid-19 vaccine has just been released. Some people can't wait to get it, and others believe it's dangerous/fraudulent, etc. Those opinions have nothing to do with whether or not the vaccine is actually safe. Truth is truth, regardless of human opinion. This same principle applies to the related objection that states, "You're just a Christian because you were born in the US. If you were born in India, you'd probably be Hindu." That may well be the case, but that describes me; it has no bearing on whether or not Jesus is actually the only way to God.

It's this belief that Jesus is the only way that fuels the sharing of the Gospel (Good News) all over the world. If there were many ways to God, Christians wouldn't have to go through the exercise, and everyone could just choose their preference like they choose what flavor ice cream they prefer. But that's not what Jesus said. In fact, he commanded the opposite:

---

[83] John 14:6 NIV

Then Jesus came to them and said, "All authority in heaven and on earth has been given to me. Therefore, go and make disciples of all nations, baptizing them in the name of the Father and of the Son and of the Holy Spirit, and teaching them to obey everything I have commanded you. And surely I am with you always, to the very end of the age[84]*."*

Pastor Peter Leal Sr., Founding Pastor of Victory Church in Middlefield, CT, is quick to remind us that this is not known as "the great recommendation." No, this is the Great Commission from Jesus. It is our duty and obligation to share the Good News of Jesus Christ because it is the only way to God.

This leads us to one final objection. Because Wedding Cake Worldviews believe all religions are valid, they believe the world would be a better place if Christians did not share their beliefs with others. Just because Christians believe it, they have no right to try and convert someone else to believe.

You see the great irony in that position, right? **The critic is, in fact doing the exact thing they are objecting to: trying to convert others to their worldview.** Now *that* is an arrogant and narrow-minded position to take.

These Wedding Cake Worldviews claim a moral high ground behind a veil of "tolerance," but in truth, they are just as exclusive as a Christian or a Muslim or a Jew who believes that their view is the correct view. **It is not tolerant to believe that every religion is valid.** I don't "tolerate" pizza from my favorite pizza places. I like them all. Tolerance requires disagreement and is about how we treat those we disagree with.

If you believe that Jesus is who He says He is, there is nothing more loving you can do than share the Good News with others. Jesus is the way, the truth, and the life. It's by his sacrifice alone that our sins can be forgiven, and we can be put back into a right relationship with God. No amount of good deeds will do it. But

---

[84] Matthew 28:18 NIV

through faith, God will take away our sin, our shame, and our guilt. He'll change our heart of stone and give us a new heart. When we put our faith in Jesus, we are free, indeed.

9. Is it really necessary to be a member of a local church?

I broke my foot last night. The fifth metatarsal, to be exact. My Dad and I were enjoying a tennis match against my brother Matt and my brother in Christ, Joe. We were only down five games to one and had them right where we wanted them. I planted my foot to chase a ball, rolled my ankle, and the next thing I knew, I was on the ground grasping my foot. Ouch.

I'd picked one of the more inopportune times of the year to get injured as it was the night before Thanksgiving, and we were hosting Thanksgiving dinner for our family. There was a lot to do to get prepared, and one tiny little bone on the side of my foot threw a wrench into our plans. I don't think I'd ever even thought about this tiny bone before last night, but isn't that the way it goes? We don't notice how important every part of our body is until we injure something.

If a tiny little bone in the foot is critical, how much more so our organs? We need our organs, and our organs need us too. Here's what I mean; organs such as a heart or lungs can only survive about 4-6 hours outside of the body.[85] That's why when it comes to organ transplants, time is of the essence. The organs *must* be transplanted to live, function, and serve their purpose. **And the same can be said about us as Christians.** We *must* be planted in a local church in order to fully live, function, and serve our purpose. The Bible actually tells us that being a member of a local church is equal to being a vital organ in a body, the body of Christ. The church needs you, and you need the church.

People become disillusioned with and leave the church for many reasons, but deep down, we long for it. We long for that

---

[85] What happens to your body when you're an organ donor? | Live Science

community. We seek that connection through our "gym family" or our kid's sports team "family" or our bowling team, etc. And those groups are wonderful, but they can never fill the void that having no church life leaves. You share some common interest with those groups, but with your church, you share *the* common interest that truly matters in life. Pastor Rick Warren explains it like this in The Purpose Driven Life: "you were called to belong, not just believe[86]." The Christian life is not meant to be a solo act. **Your life purpose includes being an active, participating member in a local church.** Why does it matter?

- **Commitment**: when you see a ring on someone's finger, they are telling the world that they've committed. That commitment brings the relationship to a higher level and positions it to grow. A ring on someone's finger obviously means something completely different than "I care about them but want to keep things casual." Similarly, joining a church means something completely different than "I'm spiritual but not into organized religion." The Wedding Cake Worldviews lack this commitment.
- **Relationship**: Jim Rohn, the entrepreneur and motivational speaker, famously said that "you are the average of the 5 people you spend the most time with[87]." We understand this, and the older we get, the more we seek to surround ourselves with people who reflect our values. Any parent will affirm this principle as they tell you that they fear their kids falling in with "the wrong crowd." Does this mean that people who go to church are inherently better than those who don't? Of course not. We'll dig into that deeper, but for now consider this: a workhorse can pull around 8,000 pounds. Now you'd

---

[86] Pastor Rick Warren explains it like this in The Purpose Driven Life: "you were called to belong, not just believe."
[87] Jim Rohn quote

expect that if you had two work horses next to one another, they could pull around 16,000 pounds together. But when they work together, two workhorses can actually pull around 24,000 pounds[88]! That's what the church does for Christians. If you are trying to follow Jesus, your spiritual walk will be aided *exponentially* by surrounding yourself with other believers.

- **Service**: serving others has been scientifically proven to make people happier and even healthier. This comes as no surprise since Jesus was the ultimate servant leader. He explained that He *"did not come to be served, but to serve, and to give his life as a ransom for many."*[89] Joining a church opens the door to give meaning to your life through serving others just like you're a tool in God's hand.
- **Nourishment**- The Bible teaches us that *"man shall not live on bread alone, but by every word that comes from the mouth of the Lord.*[90]*"* Joining a church puts you in a position to be spiritually "fed" each week as you're taught lessons from God's Word (the Bible). Just as we can't eat only a couple of times a year and expect to thrive, we can't hear a sermon a couple of times a year and expect to thrive. It's about consistency, not what we do every once in a while.

You're not meant to be a spiritual recluse. But perhaps you're not a member of a church because you had a bad experience at your prior church. Maybe the members weren't friendly to you; the sermons didn't apply to current living, they only seemed interested in your money, the music wasn't your type,

---

[88] The Power of Pulling Together - America First Newsroom

[89] Matthew 20:28 NIV

[90] Deuteronomy 8:3 NIV

whatever[91]. There is a simple solution to that: find another church! You wouldn't stop eating altogether just because you had a bad meal. Every church is made up of people, so by definition, there is no such thing as a perfect church. But when you find the right Bible-based church for you, you'll know it.

When you find the right church, you'll learn that there is a difference between *going* to church and *being* the church. If you just show up as a spectator on Sunday mornings and go on your way, that's not membership. *Being* church means you are an active participating member. You'll be knit into a community like an organ transplanted in a body. You'll form deep relationships with the other "organs," and you'll have an important role to play in serving others. You won't feel like the church is only interested in your money. Rather, you'll take great joy and pride in giving to support the kingdom of God. You'll know it when you find it.

"So in Christ we, though many, form one body in Christ, and each member belongs to all the others."[92]

10. How could I ever be a member of a church? You don't know my past.

Have you ever beat yourself up over past mistakes? Do you ever look back and feel the sting of guilt or shame? If you are your own toughest critic, consider this villain from the Bible:

This individual was highly educated and was, by any measure, a high achiever. One of the areas he achieved in, unfortunately, was persecuting followers of Jesus. He actually watched over the coats of the mob that stoned Stephen, the first Christian martyr. He led violent persecution of the young church, imprisoning and calling for the execution of men and women following Jesus.

---

[91] Purpose Driven Church, Chapter 11, Rick Warren

[92] Romans 12:5 NIV

He sounds like a pretty awful guy, right? Hey, you may have made some mistakes, but at least you're not as bad as him. Can I let you in on who this villain is? Originally, he went by the name Saul of Tarsus, but you may have heard of him by his more commonly known title: SAINT PAUL! You know, the author of more than half of the New Testament. The apostle who spent the better part of his life spreading the good news of Jesus Christ and who ultimately was martyred because of it. The figure considered as important to Christianity as anyone after Jesus. That Paul!

Yes, the Apostle Paul was an intense persecutor of the early church, and you know what? God used him anyway. He was famously converted on the Road to Damascus and radically changed the direction of his life once he began following Jesus.

Time for some self-reflection. Do you really think you've done something so bad that God can't use you? You've heard of a CEO, right? That's a Chief Executive Officer. When Paul looked back on his past, he considered himself the CSO, Chief Sin Officer[93]! So I've got news for you. The Creator of the universe is NOT limited by your past. No, His Word tells us that "as far as the east is from the west, so far has he removed our transgressions from us.[94]"

To sum things up, today's pathetic "cancel culture," says that if you've ever made a misstep in your life, we'll find it and malign you. God's Word says He'll change the heart of even the chief of sinners and use them to advance the Kingdom of God. Don't ever for a second think you're too broken or that you've made too many mistakes to be valued and used by God. Seek Him to find purpose, love, and the peace that surpasses all understanding.

---

[93] 1 Timothy 1:15 paraphrased

[94] Psalm 103:12 NIV

> *"I love those who love me, and those who seek me find me"*[95]

---

[95] Proverbs 8:17 NIV

PART 7
CONCLUSION

# CHAPTER 13

COURSE CORRECTION

My heart was pounding, my jaw was clenched, and I was shaking uncontrollably. Am I having a heart attack? Oh, God, please help me. My wife called my parents and an ambulance.

After a long night at the hospital, we had our verdict; my heart was fine. I'd had a panic attack. A panic attack? How? I was 30 years old and had never experienced anything like it. But my life changed that night. Anxiety became a part of my day, with the threat of another panic attack looming in the back of my mind. Racing thoughts and a tight chest were the new normal. But what did I possibly have to be worried about? I had an amazing wife, beautiful kids, an awesome family, a good job, a roof over our head, a wonderful support system. I had it all together, and my life was great. I was happy and healthy. This anxiety made no sense on paper.

My worry was about me. My conscience was convicting me. In the back of my mind, I felt like I'd made too many mistakes in my life and done too many dumb things in my life to deserve this. So I decided to fix it. I set out to attack the problem from every angle I could, and that's just what I did. I read every book I could find on anxiety and self-improvement. I exercised daily. I began eating better. I learned breathing techniques. I tried meditation. I spoke to a therapist. I tried it all. These things all helped, but they didn't "fix" the problem.

Finally, I got some advice from a dear friend that changed everything. This friend knew that the panic attacks had totally thrown me for a loop, taking a physical and mental toll on my body. He explained that every trial in life, big or small, is allowed by God *and if it's allowed by God, then there is a purpose.* My friend actually encouraged me to thank God specifically for the anxiety. Thank Him that He's going to use it for my good. Even if it gets worse, thank Him for it. Thank Him? Really? Thank him for the worst thing in my life? Thank Him for this thing that encroaches on my peace every day? It was a challenging message to understand at the time.

This dear friend also got me a Bible. He knew that I believed in God and went to church on Sundays, but I wasn't one to read the Bible or anything. He had me start with the Gospel of Matthew and just read a chapter or so each morning. I did, but the anxiety didn't stop. I kept reading each day for months and kept battling, but the anxiety didn't magically disappear.

One night I could feel a panic attack coming on. That familiar feeling was building up, and I knew it was coming. I told my wife I was going down to the basement to try some deep breathing to calm down. It didn't help. I was about to go back upstairs, resigned to the fact that this panic attack was coming when I saw my Bible in its usual spot. I was in the act of standing up to go upstairs, that something told me to open it and read. I'd been reading for months, so I just opened it up to where my bookmark was from the day before. And then I started crying. Out of the ~1,200 pages of the Bible, I could have opened it up to anything, but I opened it up to this:

Do Not Worry

Then Jesus said to his disciples: "Therefore I tell you, do not worry about your life, what you will eat; or about the body, what you will wear. For life is more than food, and the body more than clothes.

Consider the ravens: they do not sow or reap; they have no storeroom or barn; yet God feeds them. And how much more valuable you are than birds! Who of you by worrying can add a single hour to your life? Since you cannot do this very little thing, why do you worry about the rest?

Consider how the wild flowers grow. They do not labor or spin. Yet I tell you, not even Solomon in all his splendor was dressed like one of these. If that is how God clothes the grass of the field, which is here today, and tomorrow is thrown into the fire, how much more will he clothe you, you of little faith! And do not set your heart on what you will eat or drink; do not worry about it. For the pagan world runs after all such things, and your Father knows that you need them. But seek his kingdom, and these things will be given to you as well.

Do not be afraid, little flock, for your Father has been pleased to give you the kingdom. Sell your possessions and give to the poor. Provide purses for yourselves that will not wear out, a treasure in heaven that will never fail, where no thief comes near and no moth destroys. For where your treasure is, there your heart will be also."[96]

I experienced the love of the living God. The God of the Bible. The King of kings. I knew it was Him, and He reassured me. I experienced first-hand why the scripture says that "the Word of God is active and alive, sharper than any two-edged sword[97]." **It changed everything.**

---

[96] Luke 12:22-34 NIV

[97] Hebrews 4:12 NIV

CHAPTER 14

THE PLACE OF VICTORY

When things are going well in our lives, we can so easily fall into the trap of believing we're in control. It's an illusion. I had the weight of the world on my shoulders because I felt like I was mostly responsible for my success. Things were good, and I felt like I was good, but in the back of my mind I knew something was missing. It took the panic attacks to bring me to my knees. I believed in Jesus, but it took the anxiety for me to finally say, "God, I can't do this on my own. I need you, Jesus. I'm putting my trust in you and you alone". And that is the place of Victory! Paradoxically, **the place of surrender is the place of Victory**[98]! Surrendering my life to Jesus sparked a spiritual growth spurt and provided the ultimate course correction.

Here's how my dear friend describes it. I looked at my life like it was a wheel. I was the center of that wheel, and the various aspects of my life like my family, career, interests, and even God were spokes on the wheel. God was a part of my life, but He was just a spoke on the wheel. Mostly a Sunday morning spoke. I didn't have a relationship with Him where I could talk to Him

---

[98] Pastor Peter Leal, Sr., Founding Pastor of Victory Church in Middletown, CT.

throughout the day and feel connected. When things were rolling along smoothly, this seemed to be working just fine. It took the pain of the panic attacks to get me to move God to the center of my wheel. Now, rather than being a spoke in my wheel, it's more like God is a telescope. I see every other aspect of my life through the lens of Jesus. And it's a beautiful thing. It's the spiritual adventure of a lifetime, and I'm just getting started.

I couldn't see it at the time, but God's fingerprints are all over those panic attacks. His plans are better than our plans. My friend was right; I should have been thanking Him all along because, I needed those panic attacks to draw me out of a Wedding Cake Worldview and into a relationship with the living God.

CHAPTER 15

YOUR TURN

Jesus Christ has made Himself known to billions of people throughout history[99]. He's made himself known to people in every culture on every continent of our planet. Thousands of years after his earthly life, he remains the most influential person in history. He is the son of God and truly God in the flesh.

Our journey through this book was an exercise to strengthen our faith and prove that it's far from blind faith. But head knowledge alone won't save us. We don't need to understand the Big Bang Theory or Moral Law to know that God is real. We just need to know Him. My experience with the living God showed me without a shadow of a doubt that He is alive, and he loves me. And you know what? He loves you too. The Bible tells us that.

We know that we are all sinners and that no amount of good deeds can "earn" our way into heaven. Jesus is the way, the truth, and the life. We are called to turn away from the path we're on, even if it's a good path, and instead, believe the Good News of Jesus Christ. When we do that, our hearts are changed because we are spiritually born again. So if you've not surrendered your life to Jesus, there is no time like the present

---

[99] Case for Christ, Chapter 14, Lee Strobel

to taste and see that He is good. If you're ready, you can pray this prayer and change your life right here right now.

Lord God, I'm a sinner. I'm sorry, and I'm asking for your forgiveness. Jesus, I believe that you died on the cross for my sins, and that you defeated death by rising again. I'm turning away from my sins, and I invite you into my heart, into my life. I trust you and I make you my Lord and Savior. I will never be the same. In Jesus mighty name. Amen.

If you've just given your life to Jesus, I want to congratulate you. The next step is to find a good Bible-based church near you and get planted with other believers. Don't delay. Now buckle your seatbelt because you're in for the ride of your life. I'm praying for you.

> *Sharing the Good News of Jesus Christ is the single most loving thing you can do for someone else. In fact, Jesus commands us to continue his mission and share the good news with all nations. You have an opportunity to do that right now. If you enjoyed You Don't Need a Ph.D. to Find G-O-D, you can help others find God by leaving a review on Amazon. Positive reviews are a huge help to search results and credibility so other people can find this book. Thank you and God Bless!*
>
> *-James Finke*

Looking for more biblically based encouragement? You can sign up for James' free Good News Only Friday newsletter here: Click Here to Subscribe.

RESOURCES FOR A DEEPER DIVE

If God has sparked within you a hunger to learn more about Christianity, the list below is a literary feast for your enjoyment. I'm thankful to each one of these authors who have helped a "regular guy" like myself strengthen my faith and grow closer to God.

I Don't Have Enough Faith to be an Atheist by Norman L. Geisler and Frank Turek

The Purpose Driven Life: What on Earth am I here for? By Rick Warren

Stealing from God: Why Atheists need God to make their Case by Frank Turek

Cold-Case Christianity: A Homicide Detective Investigates the Claims of the Gospels by J. Warner Wallace

God's Crime Scene by J. Warner Wallace

More Than a Carpenter by Josh McDowell and Sean McDowell

77 FAQ's about God and the Bible by Josh McDowell and Sean McDowell

The Reason for God: Believe in an Age of Skepticism by Timothy Keller

Confronting Christianity: 12 Hard Questions for the World's Largest Religion by Rebecca McLaughlin

Mere Christianity by C.S. Lewis

Tactics: A Game Plan for Discussing Your Christian Convictions by Gregory Koukl

Faith is for Weak People: Responding to the Top 20 Objections to the Gospel by Ray Comfort

They Like Jesus but not the Church: Insights from Emerging Generations by Dan Kimball

Reasonable Faith by William Lane Craig

ABOUT THE AUTHOR

James Finke is a Christian, husband, father, businessman, and author. For years, James has been driven to study the evidence for God. A gifted storyteller, James has always enjoyed writing, but had no intention to author a book. James has no Ph.D., is not a pastor, not a scientist, and had never written a book before. Thankfully, the Creator of the universe is not limited by formal credentials and uses "regular" people for His glory. What James thought was a study to strengthen his own faith was training to share the Good News of Jesus Christ with others. Find James on Facebook at @authorjamesfinke.

Https://www.authorjamesfinke.com
Https://www.facebook.com/authorjamesfinke
Https://www.instagram.com/authorjamesfinke

I dedicate his book to my wife, Tiffany. It wouldn't exist without you. I love you more every day.

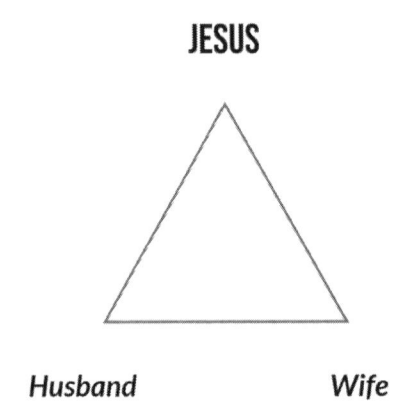

JESUS

△

Husband   Wife

Thank you to our pastor, Pastor Peter Leal, Sr., for teaching us that a lifetime of striving for Jesus is what draws us closer together.

ACKNOWLEDGMENTS

Special thank you to Laurie Labieniec and Christen Sousa, the prayer warriors for this book. We brought in the "big guns" to lift up this project. I so appreciate the care and diligence you brought to this role.

Also, only your enthusiastic feedback, wisdom, and editing notes could be longer than the book itself, Laurie. You never disappoint.

Thank you to the very talented Brooke Baker for bringing our vision for the cover to life. More of Brooke's work can be found on Instagram at bgbaker_creates.

Thank you, Joe and Melissa Labieniec. No acknowledgment could properly capture what your wise counsel, your support, and your friendship mean to Tiff and me.

Thank you, Katrina Cardillo, for the marketing and tech support, even when I interfered with your 9 PM bedtime. We're so thankful to have you and Ricky in our lives.

Thank you to our friend and "life consultant," Eleni Rock. You're truly our sister in Christ, and your support over the years is invaluable. Also, Dave is a saint.

Thank you to the entire Pastoral team at our church, Victory Church in Middlefield, CT. Eye has not seen, nor ear heard, nor have entered into the heart of man the things which God has prepared for those who love Him.

Thank you, Mom and Dad. If Tiff and I end up being half the parents that you are then we'll have done an amazing job.

Thank you, Anthony, Mia, and Abigail. You are a never-ending source of inspiration. Mom and I love you so much.

Thank you, GG, Joe, Amber, Maddy, Cam, Nate, Stace, Tyler, Ace, Amy, Matt, Bree, Deb, Jeff, Jess, Jewels, Jay, Dave, and our entire extended family.

To all of our brothers and sisters at Victory Church, thank you!

I love you all.

I also want to thank some people who I don't know personally.

I'm appreciative of the amazing Christian Apologists whose work I studied to build my own faith. There are many listed on the Deeper Dive reading list, but I'd like to highlight Frank Turek and J. Warner Wallace. Your work has helped change my life. Thank you.

I also owe a debt of gratitude to several self-publishing advocates whose work taught this first-time author how to share his message. If you have an interest in self-publishing, I strongly recommend checking out "Self-Publishing with Dale," "Kindlepreneur," and "The Courtney Project" on YouTube.

Dale also led me to "Mastering Amazon Descriptions" by Brian Meeks. That book was very helpful in showing me how terrible my first attempt at the description was. I hope it's better now!

> *All glory and praise to God. Your word never returns void. Thank You that You use us as a tool in Your hand. In Jesus' mighty name.*

Printed in Great Britain
by Amazon